T0121395

Putting Meaning
Back into Christmas for
You and Your Loved Ones

Putting Meaning Back into Christmas for You and Your Loved Ones

Elaine's Christmas Ministries
Daily spiritual readings, devotions, and poems, that build
a deeper relationship with our Savior.

By

Elaine C. Ehrich

authorHOUSE®

Information for ordering found at web sites:

AuthorHouse™ LLC
1663 Liberty Drive
Bloomington, IN 47403
www.authorhouse.com
Phone: 1-800-839-8640

© 2013 Elaine C. Ehrich. All rights reserved.

No part of this book may be reproduced, stored in a retrieval system, or transmitted by any means without the written permission of the author.

Scriptures quotes in poetry and devotions were taken from the Revised Standard Version of the Holy Bible, Old Testament Section, copyright 1952, New Testament Section copyright 1971. [2nd edition, 1971] by the Division of Christian Education of the National Council of the Churches of Christ in the United States of America. Used by permission. All rights reserved.

Published by AuthorHouse   10/29/2013

ISBN: 978-1-4817-6432-2 (sc)
ISBN: 978-1-4817-6433-9 (e)

Library of Congress Control Number: 2013910841

Any people depicted in stock imagery provided by Thinkstock are models, and such images are being used for illustrative purposes only. Certain stock imagery © Thinkstock.

This book is printed on acid-free paper.

Because of the dynamic nature of the Internet, any web addresses or links contained in this book may have changed since publication and may no longer be valid. The views expressed in this work are solely those of the author and do not necessarily reflect the views of the publisher, and the publisher hereby disclaims any responsibility for them.

About the Author

Elaine C. Ehrich has lived in the central and western United States all of her life. She has always been active in her church. Expressing her faith in poetry and in sharing it with her friends and family has had a huge influence in her life. After recent injuries she wants to share with those who are in need of support and encouragement in their lives and she gives thanks for the many blessings that she did not even think about previously.

She reads extensively, does crafts, likes painting, music, and cooking. She also enjoys traveling and has traveled most of the United States. She has traveled in Europe, the Caribbean, Canada, and Mexico. She worked as a nurse and marriage family therapist. She also did volunteer work in her communities as a drug and alcohol counselor, Sunday school teacher, parish nurse, and many other church activities.

This booklet is dedicated to everyone who gave me their support and encouragement. Also my thanks and appreciation go to everyone who shared my belief that these poems may make a difference in people's lives and provided me with the guidance I needed to continue the effort to bring these poems and devotions to those who can use them. I also thank all the pastors and those in leadership positions who gave guidance.

Christmas Poems

❦

Preface

I want to share some of the highlights that explain some of the events that helped inspire these poems. The first poem I wrote, "Good News", honors the Good News Bible and devotions for the role it played in my spiritual growth. I was inspired to share "Good News" and my other poems with those close to me, as that seemed to be why I was writing them. The feedback I got was overwhelmingly positive so I continued writing poems with a Christmas theme.

Around the mid-nineties, the morale of people living in Sacramento, Ca began to decay. Several churches were burned, articles stolen, and valued possessions deliberately broken. These crimes were also occurring where I lived and have resulted in the loss of several of my poems. Some of the hatred was directed toward people of religious faith and Christians became the target of harassment. When I wrote the poem entitled, "Jesus" there were rumors about Jesus that portrayed Christians in a negative manner, and this poem included some of the materials that surfaced at the time.

After suffering several severe injuries I was deeply affected by unexpected healing and began writing a poem that year that ended up being "My Miracle." My life changed and I became eager to share my experiences with other Christians and anyone else in need of inspiration and help. I hope that you will be inspired by reading these poems to seek Jesus, ask the Holy Spirit to increase your faith, and find the hope, joy, and love that was brought to us that first Christmas Day.

To the Reader of Elaine's Christmas Poetry and Devotions:

This book contains poems with religious themes about Christmas for the extraordinary and most wonderful gift we received on Christmas which is there, waiting for you and me to accept Him. These poems were meant to help you put true meaning back into your holidays by giving you the opportunity to read in a modality that you may not be familiar with, that of poetry. It may help bring the spirit of Christmas alive in you or in someone who is questioning how and why he feels so burdened and stressed out by our holiday celebrations. Each poem has with it six devotions that can be read weekly or daily. An individual might like to read each devotion daily. Groups or families may like to read all six on one or two nights per week or more. You might read the Christmas story and your favorite devotion with your family before opening gifts on Christmas.

There are blank pages where, if you choose, you may apply your favorite Christmas card scene or drawings to match the theme of the poem. A collage of your favorite poem might be nice if you are a family. If you choose to do this, you will have a beautifully illustrated keepsake that provides you with your own special memories of the holidays.

This book will be useful for those bringing comfort and support to others. Some who could find this book helpful are families, friends, parents, Sunday School teachers, ministers, group workers, prison workers, and anyone else involved in work with those in need of support, comfort, or growth. It can also be useful as a meditation and devotional resource for those seeking spiritual growth. There will be several blank pages at the end of the book useful for notes after reading and discussing the devotions or to track your yearly Christmas activities.

Spiritual Readings And Devotions

"Good News"

Share the good news this Christmas
With someone who's seeking a need,
And he will find peace and contentment
In the following messages he heeds.

With Jesus, the center of Christmas,
Any problem will find its own cure,
But we foolishly forget all the things He taught us,
As we rush frantically forward once more

To spend trivial times in self-indulgences,
Which leaves little time for the message He brought,
That He is our personal Savior,
And not found in the Christmas glitter we sought.

Take time to contemplate the meaning
That the word was made flesh and through us interwove,
Then we will search and find the true meaning,
Of God's unfathomable, omnipotent love.

Jesus appears when we least expect Him,
To show us His wisdom and way,
But he expects us to obey and trust
And share the good news with others today.

There are many who don't want to hear this,
Who would postpone the lesson for tomorrow,
Who forgot the true meaning of Christmas
As they are all consumed by selfish desire or sorrow.

Share the good news this Christmas
With someone who is seeking a need,
So he may find peace and contentment
When he hears of our Savior's deeds.

Good News

Devotions for Day 1

An angel appeared to the shepherds saying, "Be not afraid; for behold, I bring you good news of a great joy which will come to all the people."

Luke 2:10

Sharing the good news of the gospel seems so simple—that a Savior was born for each and every one of us. Yet it is now over two thousand years after His birth and not every one of us has had the opportunity to have their own Bible. Those of us who live in the United States are so blessed. If one doesn't own a Bible it is not difficult to find one.

Our forefathers planned to bring education to every person living here. Because of this blessing, we can read our Bibles for ourselves. How many of us read our Bibles daily and thank our Lord and Savior for these opportunities? Those who have paved the way fought for the freedom of being able to read, write, and worship. However, the freedom to worship has eroded into the rights to not worship as nonbelievers, atheists, and skeptics have become stronger in declaring those freedoms for themselves. For example, schools and nursing homes are being told they no longer have the right to honor the name of Jesus with religious literature in group rooms. Is this the work of Satan in our nation? Our founding fathers never intended the separation of church and state to go this far. Have we forgotten to ask the Lord's guidance for our daily walk through life? Who will you choose to follow, and by not taking any action, have you not already chosen?

Prayer:

Lord, you have given each of us different gifts that can be used to spread the good news such as the gift to write, to organize, and to communicate. Help us use these special skills to serve you; and reach out to those who don't have Bibles. Amen.

Good News

Devotions for Day 2

"And we will bring you the good news that what God promised to the fathers, this he has fulfilled to us their children by raising Jesus."

Acts 13:32-33

In this present day, our nation is being faced with many challenges. Our nation is built on the motto, "In God we trust," but it is being led further and further from the guidance of the Lord. Our schools teach more about other religions, I hear, then they do about Christianity and how that may be applied to our daily lives. Now, I grant you that religious upbringing has its main source in the church or one's family. This allows the schools to focus on teaching other matters and subjects! But will God be there for us if we allow ourselves to dishonor Him through avoidance of His name?

God has delivered our nation from many perils over the years, but it is now facing many internal disagreements. "On him we have set our hope that he will deliver us again" (2 Corinthians 1:10). Our children are spending half of their day in schools where they cannot share the good news if an occasion arises and where they cannot pray with other Christians about a need that presents itself. Should we continue to be led by a legal community that denies us this right to honor Jesus when an opportunity arises? In Joshua, we are taught, "And if you be unwilling to serve the Lord, choose this day whom you will serve,—but as for me and my house, we will serve the Lord" (24:15).

Prayer:

Lord, our days become so busy that we forget to find you in them. Worst of all, we forget to grasp the opportunities to share the good news with others that come into our lives. We ask for your mercy in our unbelief and lack of actions. Amen.

Good News

Devotions for Day 3

"Go therefore and make disciples of all nations, baptizing them in the name of the Father and of the Son and of the Holy Spirit."

Matthew 28:19

One can understand the Trinity as a wholeness. But it has helped me to think of each part of the Trinity as having a job to do in bringing this good news to each and everyone of us. God created us in His image with free-will. God blessed humankind and gave us all authority to govern this earth, including all animals, all living things in the oceans, and everything that lives on this earth. But everything belongs to God and in our stewardship we honor Him by living for Jesus. Jesus came to earth to bring the good news of God's unending love for us and to bring forgiveness of our sins. Jesus told His disciples, "I am the way, and the truth, and the life; no one comes to the Father, but by me" (John 14:6). We often want to deny, to escape, or to hide from the decision to accept Jesus as our Savior, which happens when we harden our hearts to His word. But if we respond to God's love and accept Jesus as our Savior, the Holy Spirit can work within us to help us grow in faith, making us spiritually alive. Jesus said, "You did not choose me, but I chose you" (John 15:16). So we each are called to play a different part in sharing the good news with others.

Prayer:

Let us be open to the Holy Spirit working in our lives. Keep us in your joy and peace. Help us share and spread your good news to others who have not heard about your coming to this earth and dying to deliver us from our sins. Amen.

Good News

Devotions for Day 4

[Jesus] said, "Go into all the world and preach the gospel to the whole creation."

Mark 16:15

The apostles were sent by Christ to bring His good news to all who would receive it. Christ said to them, "you shall be my witnesses in Jerusalem and in all Judea and Samaria and to the end of the earth" (Acts 1:8). This news of His forgiveness of sins by faith in His death and resurrection has affected more lives and changed more history than any other recorded event.

As our knowledge and technology have increased, some have found it more difficult to continue to believe. They may even become scoffers like Saul. Following his conversion, Saul was transformed by the Lord into Paul, one of Christ's hardest working apostles. What a miracle occurred when Paul accepted Christ. He had been a leader of the persecution of the church. After Saul's conversion, Christians went everywhere in the dispersion caused by Saul, and they told the story of Jesus Christ, our Savior. In many of the New Testament books, one reads about the beatings, stoning, imprisonment, and other persecutions Paul went through to spread the good news. At that time, the Roman military had built new roads, and these roads served the growth of Christianity well. The good news about Christ could spread more quickly.

Prayer:

Jesus, let us be open to opportunities to share the good news. Thank you for the opportunities you have given us and help us take action on them even during the busy time of Christmas. Help us keep our priorities straight, with you first in our lives. Amen.

Good News

Devotions for Day 5

[Jesus] "went on through cities and villages, preaching and bringing the good news of the kingdom of God".

Luke 8:1

Most of us do not become great evangelists, but we can affect those around us by our witness for Christ. We hear of teenagers who helped out classmates in need, but most of these stories do not get shared. We have read in newspapers and seen on television people who are possessed by some derangement of mind, who belong to some cult, or who perform acts such as murder, robbery, or other criminal acts against others while on illegal drugs. How does this mass communication that spreads over states and countries affect our daily living for Christ when so much of the news is negative? Jesus often went away in order to pray and to be strengthened and refreshed. We are to do likewise. Jesus taught Martha, "You are anxious and troubled about many things; one thing is needful. Mary has chosen the good portion, which shall not be taken away from her" (Luke 10:41-42).

Jesus taught, "But seek first his kingdom and his righteousness" (Matt 6:33). Today we have opportunities to share. Tomorrow this opportunity to spread the good news may not be there. Just as Satan worked in the life of Jesus from the time of His birth to His resurrection Satan is constantly working to close these doors. Paul says, "for even Satan disguises himself as an angel of light" (2 Corinthians 11:14). Jesus overcame Satan, and it is only through His name and teachings that we remain in the love, joy, and peace brought to us by the little baby Jesus.

Prayer:

Lord, help us to reach out to our Christian teenagers, as they seem most vulnerable to the immorality that our nation has been facing. Let our witness be used by you to bring teenagers to Christ, as we attempt to involve them in meaningful service at Christmas. Let us share the gospel with others to your honor and glory. Amen.

Good News

Devotions for Day 6

The angel said to Zechariah, "I am Gabriel, who stand in the presence of God; and I was sent to speak to you, and to bring you this good news."

Luke 1:19

The Old Testament ended with the prophecy that Elijah would come to earth again. The New Testament story in Luke begins with Gabriel's news to Zechariah. Gabriel appears to tell Zachariah, a priest, that his elderly, barren wife would have a son to whom that prophecy pointed. This baby was to be named John. Jesus later said, "he is Elijah who is to come" (Matthew 11:14). John the Baptist, as he is called, came to prepare the way for Jesus. "For you will go before the Lord to prepare his ways" (Luke 1:76). The time was at hand for Jesus Christ, the Messiah, to come!

The good news was spread by angels, by signs in the sky, and through other supernatural events. People then did not have cable or computers, but the news traveled quickly among those watching over the eastern area with expectations for the signs of the coming Messiah. Then an angel appeared to Mary to tell her, a virgin, that she was the chosen one to carry and give birth to Jesus. This supernatural event was proceeded by yet another, even greater miracle still to come: that of the resurrection of Jesus.

Prayer:

Lord, help us to see the entire picture of any event as you do. Grant that we accept and search out opportunities for increased patience while serving you. We thank you for the miracles that you brought, especially the birth of Jesus Christ and we pray for your guidance in our life to keep Christmas meaningful each year. Amen.

Spiritual Reading and Devotions

"A Christmas Message In the Dark of the Night"

The story of Christmas is not complete

Without the news spoken in the dark of night by the angel,

Appearing to shepherds who were without conceit,

Bringing news of the birth, Lord Emanuel.

The shepherds were on a nearby hill

That night watching over their special flock,

When a bright light appeared in the dark night's chill,

Leaving them frightened, in awe and shock.

Heard in the dark of night the voice of the angel clear,

Telling them of the birth of a baby adored,

No questioning or thinking, "Did I mishear?"

Nor was the angel's message ignored.

These shepherds heard the good news:

As poor as they were, a Savior was born to them,

Selected to honor Him even though in number few,

Remembering the angel's song, that they came not to condemn.

A birth of a Savior was long expected

Among the Jewish scribes and historian foretold;

The angels did not leave the shepherds undirected,

Bringing a message for all men, none left out in the cold.

These shepherds, who were poor and lowly,
Did not question the message the angel had brought;
Having faith, they hurried, not going slowly,
To find in Bethlehem, the Babe, Jesus Christ, whom they sought.

The shepherds knew what a great event occurred and took heed,
They praised and glorified God, King of Kings,
And the news of that night's events has spread indeed,
Leaving all to ponder the Babe, and God's praises to sing.

But then I wonder how I would behave
If among the shepherd I did abide;
Could I be faithful and brave,
Or would I from the hills flee and hide?

How would this change the Christmas story,
Given no response to the angel's song,
With no response of one of lowly status to honor
The Babe, Lamb of God, brought to earth to show God's love so strong?

And the Angels appeared telling the shepherds of the Good News.

Christmas Message In the Dark of the Night

Devotions for Day 1

"And suddenly there was with the angel a multitude of the heavenly host praising God and saying, "Glory to God in the highest, and on earth peace among men with whom he is pleased!""

Luke 2:13-14

Christmas is a time of much joy. At last, the long-prophesied birth of a Savior for Israel had occurred. And to announce His birth, angels, special messengers of God, appeared to the shepherds near Bethlehem. They announced that His birth was good news, not just for Israel but for all people. So, all are included in this Christmas message.

According to tradition there were special flocks in the area that were used for sacrifices in the temple. The shepherds, to whom the angels appeared, may have been the ones assigned to these special flocks. The animals used for sacrifices in the temple had to be without blemish. Does this not describe Jesus? "For our sake he made him to be sin who knew no sin" (2 Corinthians 5:21). What love and caring God showed to us all by bringing His Son to this sinful world! I wonder how much the shepherds understood of this message and how much was revealed to them of the price this little baby would pay to show us a better way to live. No longer would sacrifices in the temple be required of the people. Jesus Christ's sacrifice was so loving, so pure, and so ultimate that it continues to change the hearts of men and women even today. Seek ways to share this book with others at Christmas.

Prayer:

Dear heavenly Father, we thank you for the Christmas greeting brought by your messengers to the shepherds that dark night near Bethlehem. The life of that little baby, your Son, has changed this world as no one else has done. I invite Him into my heart where He can change my sinful nature, make me less prideful, and more loving to all humankind. Amen.

A Christmas Message In the Dark of the Night

Devotions for Day 2

"There were shepherds out in the field, keeping watch over their flock by night."

Luke 2:8

There was an immense number of sheep raised in Palestine during this time. The number of sheep could vary from several thousands or more per flock. Characteristically, sheep tend to stray away and are not as easily led as is assumed. "For you were straying like sheep, but have now returned to the Shepherd and Guardian of your souls" (I Peter 2:25). During the night there can be much danger for the sheep. So, depending upon the weather and presence of wild animals, such as bears, lions, or wolves, the shepherds may have brought their sheep that night to a sheepfold, which is a natural enclosure where a band of shepherds can prevent animals from sneaking into the flock. Also, if a sheep was found missing, the shepherd could go look for it, leaving his sheep with the others. Jesus tells us, "What man of you, having a hundred sheep, if he has lost one of them, does not leave the ninety-nine in the wilderness, and go after the one which is lost, until he finds it?" (Luke 15:4).

That night, Jesus came to earth as a little baby, because he cared for each of us and wants to find us, his lost sheep. "There is joy before the angels of God over one sinner who repents" (Luke 15:10). Knowing this, the angels brought great tidings of joy to the shepherds. When our focus is on Jesus at Christmas we, also, have the joy the shepherds experienced.

Prayer:

Help us to remain humble in your forgiveness and in faith. And thanks to you, God, for sending us your Son as our Savior and for clearly showing us the love and care He has for us. Amen.

A Christmas Message In the Dark of the Night

Devotions for Day 3

"Has not the scripture said that the Christ is descended from David, and comes from Bethlehem, the village where David was?"

John 7:42

Ruth, a Moabite, returned to Bethlehem with her mother in law, Naomi, after Naomi's husband and son died. About one mile east of Bethlehem there was a field thought to be the field owned by Boaz, where Ruth gleaned grain to feed herself and her mother-in-law, Naomi. It was here that Ruth and Boaz met and fell in love. They were part of the genealogical line from which Christ was to be born.

After the birth of Ruth's son, Naomi was honored by women she knew who "named him Obed; he was the father of Jesse, the father of David" (Ruth 4:17). Ruth became the great grandmother of King David. It is prophesied "But you, O Bethlehem Ephrathah, who are little to be among the clans of Judah, from you shall come forth for me one who is to be ruler in Israel" (Micah 5:2). It is believed that it was in a nearby field to the one where Ruth harvested grain that the angels appeared to the shepherds. The appearance of the angels in the night must have been awesome as the shepherds "were filled with fear" (Luke 2:9). In this same field, David may have tended his father's flocks as a young boy and may have written some of his psalms so many years ago.

Prayer:

Lord, let us always be open to your will. We thank you for teaching us how magnificently you prepared for the birth of your Son, Christ Jesus. Help us teach this to our children and never be too proud to ask forgiveness and seek to honor you. This we ask in Jesus' name. Amen.

A Christmas Message In the Dark of the Night

Devotions for Day 4

"My sheep hear my voice, and I know them, and they follow me."

John 10:27

The Christmas message brought to the shepherds was that God loved us so much that He sent His Son to be our Savior. This Savior was just born a short distance away and would give forgiveness for our sins so that we all could have eternal life. The angel of the Lord proclaimed, "Be not afraid; for behold, I bring you good news of a great joy which will come to all the people" (Luke 2:10).

In John 10, Jesus tells us about the art of shepherding and what it was like to be a shepherd in Palestine. Shepherding may consist of driving the sheep, but when a shepherd first goes out of the sheepfold and calls his sheep by their names, they will follow him. Jesus told them that others who came before him were like thieves, robbers, and hirelings. They saw the wolf coming and, caring nothing for the sheep, left the sheep to be scattered and killed. Jesus told them about His coming death and resurrection, "For this reason the Father loves me, because I lay down my life, that I may take it again" (John 10:17). This is what a good shepherd does for his sheep, and it is the reasons for the great joy that was brought to all. If our thoughts are on Jesus, Christmas will always be a meaningful time of the year for us.

Prayer:

Dear heavenly Father, we know that you came to earth for each and every one of us to be born of a virgin. Thank you for the love you have given us and for being our Redeemer. Amen

A Christmas Message In the Dark of the Night

Devotions for Day 5

"And this will be a sign for you: you will find a babe wrapped in swaddling cloths and lying in a manger."

Luke 2:12

The angels were inviting the shepherds to go to Bethlehem to find Jesus, their Savior. And what a spectacular invitation they received: a band of angels appearing in the sky in the darkest of hours! The shepherds were to look for a newborn baby dressed in swaddling clothes in a manger. Swaddling clothes are narrow bands of cloth put around the limbs of the baby to prevent motion; they were used to keep Jesus warm and protected, and to stop his crying which may have bothered the many people who were nearby in the crowds.

We know the shepherds were at first afraid, but as they discussed the news the angels brought, they were guided to go to Bethlehem. They probably did not wait until morning but went that very night. "And they went with haste, and found Mary and Joseph, and the babe lying in a manger" (Luke 2:16). Events leading to the birth of a Messiah had been occurring very slowly, but the shepherds knew that something important had happened, and they rushed to give honor to Jesus. Bethlehem was overflowing with people who were there for the census. The shepherds shared their news with those they met, who then returned rejoicing and thanking God. Thus, the spread of the good news had its beginning as people returned to their homes from the census. How can you and your family spread the good news this Christmas?

Prayer:

Lord, we rejoice and thank you for the news this day of the Redeemer you sent to us on that first Christmas morning. We know how much we need Him in our lives. We ask that you guide us to find ways to extend the angels' invitation to others. Amen.

A Christmas Message In the Dark of the Night

Devotions for Day 6

"For to you is born this day in the city of David a Savior, who is Christ the Lord."

Luke 2:11

The angels greeting to the shepherds declared fulfillment of the prophecy that a Savior would be born in Bethlehem. Some historians write that the place where Jesus was born, might have been beneath the Church of the Nativity. Some also speculate that is where the home of Boaz and Ruth was once located. We know that this city, the birthplace of Jesus, is filled with important historical events; it is where many miraculous occurrences happened as God attempted to let humankind know Him more personally. At long last, a baby, true God and true man, had come to reveal God to humans.

It was prophesied that the Messiah would be born of a virgin. Isaiah said, "Behold, a young woman shall conceive and bear a son, and shall call his name Immanuel" (Isaiah 7:14). When the angel appeared to Mary with news that she would be the mother of Jesus, she said, "How shall this be, since I have no husband?" (Luke 1:34). What faith and obedience the Lord found in this woman as she responded, "let it be to me according to your word" (Luke 1:38). Jesus taught, "If you have faith as a grain of mustard seed, you will say to this mountain, 'Move from here to there,' and it will move; and nothing will be impossible to you" (Matthew 17:20).

Prayer:

We give thanks that our Savior has come to earth, to bring us His love, peace, joy, and salvation. Let us open ourselves to the teachings of Jesus to receive understanding and hope. May the Holy Spirit increase our faith and use this book to help make Christmas meaningful to those who are in doubt and questioning. Amen

Spiritual Readings and Devotions

"The Brightest Star"

Someplace to the east of Jerusalem
Wise men saw in the heavens; a new star;
To where Jesus was it led them,
With gold, frankincense, myrrh brought from afar.

What was this shining star so bright
That seemed to move across the sky?
It was such a beautiful sight;
Did it represent Jesus nearby?

One is left to wonder and speculate
On how such a star came to be;
It's in the mysteries of what God did create
And not just in one's fantasy.

Was Jesus the star from Jacob
Who was predicted to come?
Was that the connection of what God did create,
And the birth of Jesus, our Savior to become?

Some say the star was a comet bringing good will;
Others think it a spaceship moving in the sky so free.
There are also those who think the earth stood still,
So Jesus could be worshipped by royalty, the wise men three.

But I know in my heart,
Whatever it was the bright star was part of God's plan,
To bring His love to earth to impart,
The Good Tidings of love and peace to deliver to man.

The Brightest Star

Devotions for Day 1

"And lo, the star which they had seen in the East went before them, till it came to rest over the place where the child was."

Matthew 2:9

The Bible does not tell us where the wise men came from but it is assumed that they came from Persia. "Behold, wise men from the East came to Jerusalem" (Matthew 2:1). Ancient authors applied the term wise men to a class of priests from Persia and Medes. It was a term that was later applied to all eastern philosophers. Throughout East Asia, men were looking for a child who was to come from heaven, restore Israel to its former glory and power, and bring forgiveness of sins. They may have gained this knowledge from the Jews, such as Daniel, who had been one of the captives living in that region.

Astrologists have tried to explain the event as a nova or as the conjunction of Jupiter and Saturn, which occurred near the time of the birth of Jesus, that would account for the brightest star. However, none of these account for the phenomena of a moving star. The miracle of the star and the miracle of Jesus' birth both occurred at approximately the same time. Jesus said, "I am the root and offspring of David, the bright morning star" (Revelation 22:16). He alone is the one to whom this prophecy pointed.

Prayer:

Dear Lord, thank you for coming to earth bringing us your love and redemption. Let us be secure in our faith that the Holy Spirit will continue His works within us. We seek your will in finding ways to make Christmas meaningful each year as we focus on Jesus. Amen.

The Brightest Star

Devotions for Day 2

"A star shall come forth out of Jacob, and a scepter shall rise out of Israel".

Numbers 24:17

Balaam, who had the gift of prophesy and divination, was the one who gave the prediction read in Numbers 24:17. King Balak, of the Moabites, hired Balaam to curse the Israelites because they were camped on the border of his land and he was afraid of them, but God intervened, and Balaam gave a blessing to them instead. Part of this blessing was that out of Jacob's lineage was to come a Savior, a Messiah, and a Star who would bring hope to the Israelites and who would die to save us all from our sins.

His prophesy also used the word *scepter*, which means staff. It predicted one with great power was to come out of Israel. It was also a word applied to a shepherd's rod. So the star, unexplainable in terms of the known natural laws of humankind, was the miraculous announcement of the birth of Jesus Christ, our Savior, leading the wise men to the exact place where Jesus was born in Bethlehem. Jesus said, "I am the good shepherd. The good shepherd lays down his life for the sheep" (John 10:11).

Prayer:

Guide us, Lord, in our daily walk through this life as the Star guided the wise men to you, in Bethlehem, so many years ago. You alone are worthy of the name of the Good Shepherd. You are indeed, our awesome Savior. Help us to be patient and wait upon your answers to our prayers. Help us to be a blessing to others especially during this coming Christmas. Amen.

The Brightest Star

Devotions for Day 3

"The people who walked in darkness have seen a great light."

Isaiah 9:2

Isaiah prophesies of a great light, which is the coming of Jesus Christ's birth. In Isaiah 9:6, Jesus is called "Wonderful Counselor, Mighty God, Everlasting Father, Prince of Peace." What a tribute Isaiah gave to Jesus as he was directed to honor Him by God. Through the centuries, we have centered our worship on this light.

Many hymns have words that show the importance of the brightest star in our worship of the Christ child. The "Brightest and Best of the Stars" is a hymn that tells of guiding the wise men to where the infant Redeemer was laid. Gifts and offerings of respect and worship were brought by the wise men. But they also brought one other gift, the best and richest gift: our hearts' adoration. That is the gift Jesus has most wanted from all of us. Does Jesus have your love and adoration? How do you show this at Christmas? Perhaps reading the poems and devotions with your family starting about the first of November will get you ready for your Christmas celebration.

Prayer:

Dear heavenly Father, by the star of the east you revealed your Son to all the people of this world, and gave us opportunities to know you through the presence of your Son, Jesus Christ. May we worship Him with all our love and gladness as we grow in a closer relationship with our Lord, our Counselor, the Mighty God, the Everlasting Father, the Prince of Peace. Amen

The Brightest Star

Devotions for Day 4

"I am the root and the offspring of David, the bright morning star."

Revelation 22:16

Stars have played important roles in getting the Christmas story out to the world. A new star appeared in the sky where the wise men lived. This star helped bring the story of the birth of Jesus Christ to the people of the Orient. They knew it meant the long expected Messiah was born, and their faith was rewarded, as it led them to his birthplace. Another message seems to be indicated here in Revelation. The morning star can be seen best at dawn, just as it is getting light. Possibly, this is a reminder to all of us that we, too, should seek Jesus each morning. Is it easier to find Him when our minds are not yet cluttered with daily chores and activities? If we spend time with Jesus in prayer or reading his word in the morning, we can readily ask Him to go with us on our day's journey.

We are also face-to-face with the ultimate truth. Jesus Christ is the one true, the only Savior. He is the one talked about and foreseen in the Old Testament. His coming fulfilled all prophesy, and He came to forgive the sins of all. His invitation is to come to Him, to take the water of life, and to rest in Him. He is our one and only hope. Let us seek through prayer and meditation how Jesus wants us to make Christmas meaningful each year.

Prayer:

Dear Lord, we can so easily be tossed and turned each day as we face the struggles that you have given us. We ask that you be by our side and intercede for us. Make our faith strong for the tasks given us. We thank you for coming to this earth to die, to grant us forgiveness of all our sins, and for bringing love, hope, and peace daily to each of us. Amen.

The Brightest Star

Devotions for Day 5

"When they saw the star, they rejoiced exceedingly with great joy."

Matthew 2:10

The wise men had traveled miles to get to Jerusalem. Part of their travel had been through the hot desert sands. In these early centuries, many bandits were hiding, waiting to attack travelers, so they had probably joined a larger caravan crossing the desert as that was much safer than just a few traveling alone. They had to carry with them a means of payment for the supplies they needed so they would have been an easy prey if precautions were not taken.

The wise men might have felt an urgency to locate Jesus as they have been searching and waiting for His coming for many years. Their faith must have been great for them to follow a moving star which led just them to the birthplace of Jesus. Their rejoicing must have been heard by those nearby as it states their joy was great. What is not mentioned is if others could also see the moving star. Certainly, a moving star would have caused much fear or excitement among the nations or fellow travelers. There seems to be no mention of this phenomena in history books. The star, seems to be the light of some supernatural cause, appearing as directed by God to tell of the birth of Jesus Christ, True God and True Man, to the wise men. Let us follow our hearts, this Christmas. A Christmas event I remember was a caroling session that lifted the spirit of my heart, honored God, and had some of the best pianist music ever heard. What events brought the meaning of Christmas to you?

Prayer:

Dear heavenly Father, I believe, help my unbelief and increase my faith so that I can have faith as strong as the wise men. Help me make Jesus number one in my life. Amen.

The Brightest Star

Devotions for Day 6

"Praise him, sun and moon, praise him, all you shining stars!"

Psalms 148:3

All creation is attuned to praising God. All nature shows the wisdom and love that God put into His plan for this universe. This includes the star that led the wise men of the east to Bethlehem, where they found the baby Jesus in the stable. Was this star planned to appear at the fullness of time? Yes, God had planned the exact moment in history that His Son, Jesus Christ, would be born, and the appearance of this star was part of it.

We can allow ourselves to become skeptical and worried over what made this star work for the wise men. However, as we grow in faith and obedience, we question less and hang on for the glorious ride that God takes us on. Many times things don't make sense, but tasks and events appear to be put in our pathway to help us grow spiritually. So we praise God for sending His Son, Jesus Christ, to this earth. He came in perfect obedience so we would no longer be in bondage to the sacrifices of the Old Testament. In grace, we again become the children of God when we receive forgiveness of our sins. We are restored to all the benefits of being His children. This Christmas, let's talk about the many gifts each one of us received from Jesus.

Prayer:

We praise you Lord, for this beautiful universe you have given us to live in. As we become more aware of nature we see more and more examples of how perfect you made this earth. We bring our worries about the weather, disasters, and effects of war to you seeking how you want us to care for this world. Amen.

Spiritual Readings and Devotions

"Christmas Season"

Jesus, our Savior, was born when Mary and Joseph traveled far,

To Bethlehem, where God gave Him a special star,

So shepherds could come from the nearby hills,

And wise men would bring gifts to help pay for the bills.

Christmas is a time of great joy:

When Jesus came to earth as a baby boy,

This is a special time to celebrate His birth,

Which we do by sharing our love and mirth.

He came to show us all a higher way

And bring tidings of peace and good-will the angels say.

He had you in mind when Jesus came;

Jesus wants to know that we all love Him the same.

So spend a little of your time this busy season,

And you will find out the Christmas reason.

Tell Jesus that you love Him for what He's done,

And the meaning of Christmas will be clear, my son.

Christmas Season

Devotions for Day 1

"And they fell down and worshiped him. Then, opening their treasures, they offered him gifts, gold and frankincense and myrrh."

Matthew 2:11

The wise men had been traveling months by camel to locate Jesus, and the star led them to the exact place where Jesus was. They brought gifts which included the precious resins or oils of myrrh and frankincense, which were used in incense and in perfumes. Frankincense was used in sacrificial fumigation. Myrrh was used in the purification of women. Now Jesus and His family had the means to participate in the ceremonial sacrifices and purification acts that were required of Jews at the temple.

Soon, after the visit of the wise men, it was thought that Herod issued a decree to kill all males up to the age of two in the area. He was determined he would have no competition for his job. Could the purpose of the wise men's visit be to also provide money to keep Jesus safe during His childhood? The gold, which the wise men brought, probably provided lodging, donkey, and other family necessities during their time in Egypt. The angel of the Lord appeared to Joseph in a dream directing him to take Jesus to Egypt, where He would be safe from King Herod. They lived in Egypt until King Herod died, fulfilling Hosea 11:1 which states, "out of Egypt I called my son." Then, an angel of the Lord again appeared in a dream to Joseph telling him to return to Israel.

Prayer:

Dear Lord, we thank you for keeping Jesus safe from the evil in King Herod's heart. Guide us through the crises and hard times in our lives. Give us the courage and faith we need to face the stress and indecisions that take their toil through needless worry. Help us to reach out for those in need of your peace and forgiveness this Christmas. Amen.

Christmas Season

Devotions for Day 2

"Where is he who has been born King of the Jews? For we have seen his star in the East, and have come to worship him."

Matthew 2:2

Jesus was born in Bethlehem because Mary and Joseph went there to be taxed; Caesar Augustus had issued a decree. Was not this part of God's plan for Israel? The wise men came to Jerusalem seeking Jesus. So, being used to royalty, they must have thought nothing of going to Herod, the King of that region, when they sought help. Herod asked the Jewish priests and scribes to find the birthplace of this king that the wise men sought. In the prophets it was found that Christ would come from Bethlehem according to Matthew 2:6, "And you, O Bethlehem, in the land of Judah, are by no means least among the rulers of Judah; for from you shall come a ruler who will govern my people Israel." But King Herod was an evil and deceptive man. He was already planning to get rid of Jesus as soon as the wise men told him where to find Him. However, God warned the wise men in a dream not to return to Jerusalem.

The birth of Jesus is centered on a story filled with the love of God for humankind. It is a story filled with intrigue, miracles, and danger. It demonstrated the tremendous faith that those involved had in God and the obedience that they showed. Without all of these people coming together at the same time, this story would not have happened. Only God, our heavenly Father, could have created such a plan and we are to share His story with others. Let's share this year at Christmas as opportunities are provided.

Prayer:

Heavenly Father, you showed clearly how much you loved us by bringing your son, Jesus Christ, to this earth. Show us how to love you more deeply. Let our joy, love, and peace show through to others the entire year. Strengthen us to resist the devil's power. Amen.

Christmas Season

Devotions for Day 3

"As the Father has loved me, so have I loved you; abide in my love".

John 15:9

On that Christmas so many years ago Jesus came to earth as a little baby bringing God's love, joy, and peace to us. Later, Jesus told His disciples what they should do if they loved Him. They should keep His commandments, especially the one to love one another as He loves us. He told them He was to die for their sins and that they should rejoice because when He returned to His Father in heaven, He would be able to send the Comforter, the Holy Spirit, to them.

Jesus Christ, our Savior, loved us so much that He gave His life on the cross. Satan thought he had won. By dying for us and then rising again, Jesus overcame Satan. We have salvation from sin by our faith in Jesus Christ through the means of grace. But Jesus wants to know that we love Him too. He said to His disciple Peter, "Do you love me?" . . . and he said to him, "Lord, you know everything; you know that I love you" (John 21:17). Human love is not the same as the love of Christ. Without faith, we cannot begin to comprehend this. But Peter was growing in his faith, and in the power of Christ's love his leadership was changing. Jesus said, "This is my commandment, that you love one another as I have loved you." (John 15:12). When we express our love to Jesus, we have, in the power of His love, the joy and peace brought to earth that first Christmas.

Prayer:

Give us the strength to persist when we fail, the courage to press on, and the wisdom we need to help spread your word. Keep us in your love, joy, and peace, which you brought to earth when you were born. Help us reach out for others that they might know you. Amen.

Christmas Season

Devotions for Day 4

"For God so loved the world that he gave his only Son, that whoever believes in him should not perish but have eternal life."

John 3:16

For some people, Christmas is the only time they go to church. They go maybe to see a relative in a play or to hear someone they know sing a solo. How sad it is to think of all the love and joy they are missing without a close relationship with Jesus Christ.

We cannot grow in joy, love, and inner peace if we do not take an active part in keeping our relationship with Jesus Christ alive and keeping stagnation out of our daily worship. One can be surrounded by apathy, even in the organized church. It has been my experience that God provides many opportunities for us to express our love for Him. Unfortunately, we do not see all of them, even when we are focused on Jesus, because we are human, and we fail often. John 3:19 says "light has come to the world, and men loved darkness rather than light, because their deeds were evil." As we grow in faith, the Holy Spirit helps us find ways to express our love for Christ, in unique fashion, which helps us keep the love for Him alive in our daily lives, not just at Christmas. Can you express your love for Jesus in a unique, creative manner this Christmas or during the year?

Prayer:

Dear Lord, we love you and ask your guidance as we seek to find unique ways to serve you. Help us show you a fraction of the deep and ever-present love you have given to us. Thank you for pastors who are not afraid to help us find creative ways to praise you. You indeed, lift my spirit. Amen.

Christmas Season

Devotions for Day 5

"You shall love the Lord your God with all your heart, and with all your soul, and with all your mind. This is the great and first commandment."

Matthew 22:37-38

One of the Pharisees was tempting Jesus, hoping to catch Him in violation of the Jewish teachings. Jesus was asked if He knew what the great commandment was in the law. His answer was that we are to love the Lord with all our hearts, souls, and minds. We are not only to love God who is good to us but, "love your neighbor as yourself" (Matthew 19:19). Jesus was our example of how to show love. He was sent to earth by God as a baby so that He would bring love, joy, and peace to each of us. Each Christmas we celebrate having received these gifts. Christmas should not be an obligation but should be considered a time of blessing, a time . . . . to be at peace with God.

Jesus later went to the cross for us, giving His total person and His life on our behalf. He justified us by faith, and we can no longer be condemned. Satan, the world, and our own guilty conscience are continually working to condemn us. But Jesus Christ, our Savior, loves us, guards us, and keeps us. We become the recipients of God's gifts: His mercy, His grace, salivation from our sins, and ultimately eternal life.

Prayer:

Dear heavenly Father, we cannot by ourselves love others as you have commanded. Only as we grow in your word can we even phantom how wonderful and forgiving the love is that you have for us. Help us to find ways this Christmas to tell some unbeliever about your love and your story which is without a doubt, the "Greatest Story Ever Told." Teach us what you want us to know. Amen.

Christmas Season

Devotions for Day 6

"There is no fear in love, but perfect love casts out fear. For fear has to do with punishment, and he who fears is not perfected in love. We love because he first loved us".

I John 4:18-19

Jesus came to this earth because our companionship with God was broken when Adam and Eve disobeyed God. God created us and loved us so much that He wanted to restore us as His children. He did, indeed, love us first. At Christmas, when celebrating His birth, we share our love with others. The following is a good question to ask ourselves: is this activity pleasing to God? If so, the time and energy we invest will more likely result in the joy, peace, and love He brought us. Joshua says, "choose this day whom you will serve, whether the gods your father served in the region beyond the River, or the gods of the Amorites in whose land you dwell; but as for me and my house, we will serve the Lord" (24:15).

It is part of our nature to rebel against authority. Most parents can relate to this. John 14:6 states that Jesus says, "I am the way, the truth, and the life; no one comes to the Father, but by me." Only through Jesus can we know our heavenly Father, His compassion, and the love He has for us. Isn't Christmas about more than just being kind? Can we make this Christmas season special by willingly sharing our love for Him with those in need and inviting them to share our celebration where they will learn about Jesus?

Prayer:

We are thankful Dear Lord, that you freed us so that we can serve you as we "gladly go rejoicing." Help us keep your commandments, be obedient, seek your will for our lives, and remember to daily thank you for restoring us as your children. Amen.

Spiritual Readings and Devotions

"The Perfect Gift"

Has not the perfect gift been sent?
All I need to do is reach out to accept;
The love my Father in heaven showed me;
When Jesus Christ was born.

Why is it so hard to see
The love that's there for you and me,
The perfect gift that was sent from heaven
On that first Christmas when Jesus was born?

If I, like the wise men,
Will seek Him diligently,
That perfect gift will be mine, you'll see:
The love that was given so freely for me.

The shepherds came from the hills,
So excited to see the perfect gift sent their way,
To find Jesus in the manger where He lay,
On that first Christmas when Jesus was born.

It was truly a gift of wisdom,
And some say truly a gift of light,
But I think it was a gift of perfect love
Sent by our Father in heaven when Jesus was born.

Why are we so quick to forget the perfect love,
The true spirit of Christmas given,
The reason the angels came to earth,
Bringing their tidings of peace and love?

It seems we search everywhere
For the perfect gift to send,
Only to find it was already given
When Jesus Christ was born.

As I see others rushing and miffed,
I wonder if they too remember,
And give thanks for the perfect gift
Given by our Father in heaven.

The Perfect Gift

Devotions for Day 1

"For by grace you have been saved through faith; and this is not your own doing, it is the gift of God".

Ephesians 2:8

What a loving, merciful, and awesome God we have. Because of the human nature we have inherited, we constantly sin. We put other things in our lives before Jesus, the Kings of Kings. We ignore works he has ordained for us to do, take his name in vain, covet our neighbor's belongings, and forget to honor our parents. We steal, commit adultery, bear false witness, and forget the Sabbath day. But Jesus sees what is in our hearts, understands our thoughts, and is here to forgive our many sins (known and unknown) when confessed. Assurance of salvation through faith brings joy and peace when we ask the Lord's forgiveness.

In the rush of Christmas, we forget all good intentions as we get caught up in the holiday spirits. We feel sorry for ourselves, hate our neighbors, grumpily give to the church's offering, and worry about many things that are insignificant if we would only focus on Jesus. But when focused on Jesus, we realize that Christ has intervened in our lives and that we are blessed to have the good news of this special, perfect gift. We ask God's help to make Jesus the center of our Christmas activities and give thanks for this wonderful gift God sent us.

Prayer:

We give thanks for the perfect gift, for the forgiveness of sins, and for covering us in your righteousness, Jesus. Forgive us for putting other things first in our lives, for all the worry, grumbling, and for taking all blessings for granted. May my life reflect that I am one of your children. Amen.

The Perfect Gift

Devotions for Day 2

Jesus said to the woman at Jacob's well, "If you knew the gift of God, and who it is that is saying to you, 'Give me a drink,' you would have asked him, and he would have given you living water."

John 4:10

This Bible story takes place in Samaria. The Samarians were despised by the Jews, but the Samarians expected the Messiah to establish His rule through them. The city of Samaria was located about thirty miles north of Jerusalem. Jesus was probably traveling in this area because John had just been imprisoned by Herod. It was not yet His time to die, and He may have been directed by God to stay out of the land Herod ruled.

Jesus did not come to earth in a violent storm; but He came on that first Christmas like dew or a gentle rain. His birth was so humble that people not concerned may not have noticed. In John 4, we have the story of the Samaritan woman at Jacob's well. Jesus is telling her that He, Jesus, is the gift of God to humankind. He has the power to give living water if she would ask. The psalmist calls God, "the fountain of life" (Psalms 36:9). Water is used in the name of the Trinity to wash away sins, as in baptism. Baptism is a rebirth of the person to a new life in God's righteousness. Isaiah 12:3 says, "With joy you will draw water from the wells of salvation." Jesus came to die for our sins and to give us forgiveness of sins. He truly gives the water of life.

Prayer:

Help us, Dear Lord, to put our trust in your saving power and grace. Increase the faith of the people in our nation, and show us your will. This we ask in Jesus name. Amen.

The Perfect Gift

Devotions for Day 3

"For the wages of sin is death, but the free gift of God is eternal life in Christ Jesus our Lord."

Romans 6:23

Sin entered our world when Adam and Eve were disobedient. Genesis 2:17 tells us, "but of the tree of the knowledge of good and evil you shall not eat, for in the day that you eat of it you shall die." In trying to fulfill the Law we become aware of how hopeless this task is on our own. But the Old Testament also told of the coming of a Messiah who would save Israel from their sins and disobedience. Jesus is this Messiah, and He restores us as His children if we trust in him. Paul identifies the perfect gift of God as eternal life in Jesus Christ our Lord.

I have heard churchgoing people say it doesn't matter what they do or say: "all I have to do is go to confession and I will be forgiven." So one can keep sinning over and over, and Christ will just keep forgiving? Jesus, born as a baby who was true man and true God, understands what powerful desires and impulses we struggle with every day. He made us perfect, but He also gave us free will, and sin entered this world. The Old Testament helps us see how God forgives if we return to serve Him and try to do better with His help. God sees what is in our hearts. What we have learned from Jesus is that we cannot serve two masters. Luke 16:13 says, "No servant can serve two masters; for either he will hate the one and love the other, or he will be devoted to one and despise the other. You cannot serve God and mammon."

Prayer:

Lord, we think we are faultless. But we are not faultless in your sight. We humbly, thank you for eternal life which we received, not of our own doing, but freely through Jesus Christ, our Lord. Let us share this news with someone who does not know Jesus this Christmas . . . Amen

The Perfect Gift

Devotions for Day 4

"And you do not have his word abiding in you, for you do not believe him whom he has sent."

John 5:38

"But I know that you have not the love of God within you."

John 5:42

Jesus healed a man on the Sabbath, which it seems that he did to get the attention of the Jewish rulers. He wanted to teach about the strict Jewish Law which, for example, allowed them to circumcise on the Sabbath, but objected to the healings He performed on the Sabbath. He also used this opportunity to further testify to them about His deity. They have searched the scripture to find the gift that Jesus brought, that of eternal life. But Jesus, who sees all, knew that their hearts were hardened and the love of God did not abide in them. Jesus says, "yet you refuse to come to me that you may have life" (John 5:40).

At Christmas, we often focus our celebration on things that are superficial instead of on the perfect gift given to us by God. We search everywhere to find the joy and peace that Jesus brought. When our hearts are turned to the baby Jesus, we find the joy, peace, and love we so desperately want in our lives and for our families. As we grow in faith we focus on Jesus. We invite Him into our hearts and all the loneliness is gone. So take time to think about the Christmas story, with all its miracles and mysteries, and how God's plan was fulfilled in Bethlehem in a lowly manger. And gives thanks!

Prayer:

Dear Lord, we pray that our Christmas will be focused on you. Fill our lives with special memories of our Christmas. Come into our hearts, Lord and cleanse them. Amen.

The Perfect Gift

Devotions for Day 5

"On that day there shall be a fountain opened for the house of David and the inhabitants of Jerusalem to cleanse them from sin and uncleanness."

Zechariah 13:1

According to Zechariah, the gift to be received from the Lord was forgiveness of sins; it would be given to all who belonged to the lineage of David and those who lived in Jerusalem. David loved the Lord with all his heart and with all his soul. He had many good qualities, but he had done wrong things in his life. He had asked for forgiveness for these sins, and he had been punished for them. Israel was a nation that was continually sinning through worshipping other gods and idols. The worship of one true God was where David was the strongest. He went directly to the Lord for his supplications, praise, and thanksgiving.

Because of this, God established a covenant with David. It was prophesied that a great king would descend from David and would establish a kingdom that would last forever. This kingdom was that of Jesus Christ. Part of God's plan was the Christmas story. Psalms 89:3-4, says, "I have made a covenant with my chosen one, I have sworn to David my servant: I will establish your descendants forever." God also made a promise to David in 1 Kings 2:4 which says, "If your sons take heed to their way, to walk before me in faithfulness with all their heart and with all their soul, there shall not fail you a man on the throne of Israel." However, because David's son, Solomon, fell to the sin of idolatry, Israel started on its way to ruin and ended its golden era.

Prayer:

Lord, we pray for the children that they will walk in faithfulness with God. Amen.

The Perfect Gift

Devotions for Day 6

"Every good endowment and every perfect gift is from above, coming down from the Father of lights with whom there is no variation or shadow due to change".

James 1:17

James doesn't name the gifts we receive but tells us that the best, most excellent, and infallible gifts are those from our God. The best example of the perfect gift would be Jesus. One of the Christmas carols we sing is "From Heaven Above to Earth I Come". It tells of the good news and great joy that Jesus brought to everyone. Through faith, we also receive gifts like salvation, eternal life, hope, peace, love, and the Holy Spirit. Faith, itself, is a gift from God. Paul tells about the gifts we receive in 1 Corinthians 12:8-10, "To one is given through the Spirit the utterance of wisdom, and to another the utterance of knowledge according to the same Spirit, to another faith by the same Spirit, to another gifts of healing by the one Spirit, to another the working of miracles, to another prophecy, to another the ability to distinguish between spirits, to another various kinds of tongues, to another the interpretation of tongues." The Spirit gives the gifts and we do nothing to deserve them.

The purpose of the Epistle of James was to improve the morality of the Jewish Christian. It would also help the new Christian adjust to his new life. James tells us that our heavenly Father does not change. He is true, constant, unfailing, and always the same. He is Everlasting! Let us find ways to honor Him that are truly meaningful to us this Christmas.

Prayer:

We thank you Lord for the perfect gift you sent to earth that first Christmas. We thank you for foreseeing all of our needs long before we know what they are. Amen.

Spiritual Readings And Devotions

"The Many Miracles of Christmas"

They had waited years for His coming,
Had looked forward to His birth,
But now so wrought up with their lives,
Few recognized Him for who He was.

But the wise men saw His star
And traveled to worship Him from countries afar.
The star led them to Palestine where it vanished,
So to the court of King Herod in Jerusalem they languished.

King Herod was filled with fear and anger;
The scribes and chief priests were called together:
"Where is this child born?" was his demand,
As he plotted evil in his heart and hand.

And the answer came by mouth,
He's to be born in the city of Bethlehem,
There! Only five miles to the south!
In the country of Judah from Jesse's stem.

The child shall become a governor,
And the Bible says Israel to rule.
And King Herod felt chills of fear,
For to be in exile he did not hold dear.

"I need to know where this child is now,"
One can almost hear him say,
"I want to come to Him and bow,"
So tell me where it is He lay.

As they left King Herod's court,
To the wise men the star did reappear,
I can hear their joy and shout,
It's the star! It's here! It's here!

For the wise men who had traveled so far,
It's another miracle you see,
To be led to the birth place of Christ,
The Savior of all humankind . . . and me.

The gifts were an answer to their prayer:
The frankincense, the myrrh, and the gold.
One wonders how they fit into God's plan,
Or was it to keep Jesus out of the cold?

And in the dream the wise men heard,
There is a danger to the life of the child.
Return quickly to your home, as warned,
To protect the babe, meek and mild.

But another miracle was also underway
When the angel appeared to Joseph to say,
"Arise! Flee to Egypt, where the child is safe
From the hand of King Herod this day."

When I hear these Christmas miracles,
I give thanks to God above,
Who sent Jesus to earth and protected Him,
That I might have tidings of hope, peace, and love.

The Miracle Of the Star

The Star!

The Star! It's here!

It's here!

The Many Miracles of Christmas

Devotions for Day 1

"And Joseph also went up from Galilee, from the city of Nazareth, to Judea, to the city of David, which is called Bethlehem . . . to be enrolled with Mary, his betrothed, who was with child."

Luke 2:4

The city of David is Bethlehem. In Bethlehem is located the Church of the Nativity which was built approximately in 327 A.D. by Constantine, the first Christian Emperor of the Roman Empire and his mother Helena according to Wikipodia.org. Its location is where some historians think that Jesus Christ may have been born.

Mary and Joseph traveled from Nazareth to Bethlehem that first Christmas, which is a distance of about one hundred miles. They had gone to Bethlehem to take part in the census ordered by the Roman Empire. Mary had no choice but to go and God protected the little unborn Jesus, whom she carried. It was prophesied that a long-expected Savior would be born in Bethlehem. The Roman decree for a census brought Jesus's family to Bethlehem, thus fulfilling this prophesy. This was another of God's miracles that made the Christmas story complete according to the teachings of the Bible.

Prayer:

We thank you for showing us the indescribable love you have for us, Lord, by sending your only Son to earth. Through Him, in faith, we are restored as your true children. Thank you for Your birth in a lowly manger and for humbling yourself so that we could have eternal life. Let our trust in you grow stronger each day. Amen

The Many Miracles of Christmas

Devotions for Day 2

"Therefore the Lord himself will give you a sign. Behold, a young woman shall conceive and bear a son, and shall call his name Immanuel".

Isaiah 7:14

Bethlehem was packed with crowds of people because of the census. Finding no room at the inn, Mary and Joseph found the only room available. It was a stable and a manger that became the birthplace of Jesus Christ. Some historians think that Mary and Joseph may have later stayed with distant relatives related to Boaz and Ruth, who had lived in Bethlehem many years before. Jesse was their grandson, and Isaiah prophesied, "There shall come forth a shoot from the stump of Jesse, and a branch shall grow out of his roots" (Isaiah 11:1).

God sent this baby Jesus to redeem us; He was indeed true God and true man. John taught, "And the Word became flesh and dwelt among us" (John 1:14). The Messiah was long expected, but nothing happened before God's time. Paul says, "But when the time had fully come, God sent forth his Son, born of woman, born under the law, to redeem those who were under the law, so that we might receive adoption as sons" (Galatians 4:4-5). The fulfilling of God's promise had occurred, and what a miraculous event it was that occurred that night.

Prayer:

We thank you for helping us to accept your plan for our redemption and for sending your Son, Jesus our Lord, to this sinful world so that we could be restored as your children. What a wonderful miracle you gave us the night you gave us your Son, called Immanuel. Help us to be a blessing to others this Christmas as we seek your will for our lives. Amen

The Many Miracles of Christmas

Devotions for Day 3

"When the angels went away from them into heaven, the shepherds said to one another, "Let us go over to Bethlehem and see this thing that has happened, which the Lord has made known to us.""

Luke 2:15

What a miracle occurred when the announcement of Jesus's birth came from a host of angels! Even the birth of an earthly prince never received such a glorious tribute. Certainly it was easy to see that something unusual was occurring. This was God's Son, the long-expected Messiah. In the above verse, angels had just announced it to the shepherds, who had a humble station in life. It was definitely God's intent that the shepherds should know, so they could go honor Him, just as it was God's intent that the wise men would find Jesus. God wants both rich and poor to know Jesus and to honor him, The Messiah was to come from the lineage of David, and this was true of Jesus. David had been a shepherd lad, possibly tending sheep from the same fields near Bethlehem. It is thought that the shepherds sent to honor Jesus, were actually very close, possibly less than one mile away from where Jesus was born.

There is much symbolism used in the story of the shepherds. Like Jesus, the shepherd is the leader of his sheep. Christian clergy are now known as "pastors" and their congregation are known as their "flocks". Flocks represent the submissive followers who are under a shepherd who protects and cares for them. In John 10:14, Jesus says, "I am the good shepherd; I know my own and my own know me."

Prayer:

Dear heavenly Father, we know that you truly cared about us. We thank you that you loved us so much that you sent your Son to earth, to die that we might have eternal life. Help us to believe. Amen.

The Many Miracles of Christmas

Devotions for Day 4

"And the angel said to her, "Do not be afraid, Mary, for you have found favor with God. And behold, you will conceive in your womb and bear a son, and you shall call his name Jesus.""

Luke 1:30-31

"But the angel said to him, "Do not be afraid, Zechariah, for your prayer is heard, and your wife Elizabeth will bear you a son, and you shall call his name John.""

Luke 1:13

There are many miracles that include the appearance of angels in the Christmas story. All the celebration of Jesus's birth is focused on a supernatural phenomenon. John's parents were beyond the child-bearing years. Jesus was to be born of a virgin. Announcements of His birth were given by angels to Mary, Joseph, Zechariah, and angels saved Him from being killed by King Herod. In Malachi 4:5, the birth of John is predicted. "Behold I will send you Elijah." The wise men came to Bethlehem by following signs in the heavens. Most of these events were foretold about in the Old Testament. What incredible events were occurring!

This was truly an event that has been planned for a long time. This plan even had its own angel, Gabriel, (Luke 1:19), who was frequently sent by God to appear, direct, and announce the events. How blessed we are to be able to read and share this story with our families each Christmas. When would be a good time to share this story? Some families include its retelling with the opening of the gifts they give to each other. This might be a good time to also read some of the poems from this book.

Prayer:

The people in the Christmas story were specifically chosen by God for their faith, obedience, and love for their heavenly Father. Dear Lord, may you grant that we have faith like theirs. Thank you for giving us the opportunity to know you better, through your Son, Jesus Christ, our Savior. Amen.

The Many Miracles of Christmas

Devotions for Day 5

"And assembling all the chief priests and scribes of the people, he inquired of them where the Christ was to be born."

Matthew 2:4

The wise men were priests of ancient Medes and Persians. They were known as astrologers and interpreters of dreams. It is thought that they first had contact with the Jews who were in captivity in that area. They apparently had a belief in one God who created all things. The World Book Encyclopedia (1979, Vol. 13, p. 44) reports that their names were Melchior, Balthazar, and Gaspar.

As they studied astrology, the Magi saw a new star, which to them represented the birth of a Jewish King. They traveled many miles to honor Jesus, stopping in Jerusalem to ask where to find Him. After much ado, King Herod told them to look in Bethlehem and, upon finding Him, to let him know so that he also could worship the child. Once on the road, "the star which they had seen in the East went before them till it came to rest over the place where the child was" (Matthew 2:9). The long search ended in much joy and gladness. There is not just one miracle that occurred in this story but many events that are considered supernatural, all working together to bring honor to Jesus. In the past, God had put these people in contact with others who believed in one God, who were made aware of a coming Messiah, and who studied the skies enough to notice a new star that ultimately lead them to Jesus.

Prayer:

God, Help us to be alert in our worshipping, seek a new closeness to Jesus, and grow in faith so that this Christmas we can help others in their understanding and service to you. You leave us in wonder and awe when we learn of your plan to restore us as your children. Amen.

The Many Miracles of Christmas

Devotions for Day 6

"And being warned in a dream not to return to Herod, they departed to their own country by another way. Now when they departed, behold, an angel of the Lord appeared to Joseph in a dream and said, "Rise, take the child and his mother, and flee to Egypt, and remain there till I tell you; for Herod is about to search for the child, to destroy him.""

Matthew 2:12-13

The coming of the Magi let all of Jerusalem know that a child of vast importance was born whose birth was prophesied in the scriptures. They not only came to worship Him but brought gifts. These gifts became quite significant, as money was needed for their flight to Egypt. With these events unfolding, it became evident that in order for this plan to work, people with special characteristics had already been prepared and chosen by God.

Sometime before Jesus was two years old, His family fled to Egypt to protect Jesus from Herod. Matthew 2:16 states that Herod, is a rage, "killed all male children in Bethlehem and in all that region who were two years old and under." This also fulfilled scripture in Matthew 2:18 which says, "A voice was heard in Ramah, wailing and loud lamentation, Rachel weeping for her children . . . because they were no more." Some of the many miracles that occurred in this part of the Christmas story were the wise men being warned in a dream not to return to Jerusalem, an angel appearing in a dream to Joseph telling him to take his family to Egypt, and the Magi traveling miles to bring gifts that could be converted to money for the trip to escape from Herod.

Prayer:

Help us, Lord, to have patience and to know that your plan is more satisfying than any quick solution we have. We seek your guidance in our lives and for our nation. Amen.

Spiritual Readings And Devotions

"Is Christmas Only for Children?"

I have often heard it said that Christmas is for children,
And I thought how sad that is.
Then I wondered as I grew older,
When is the spirit of Christmas dead?

Does Christmas die when you are no longer a child,
Say somewhere about ten or eleven,
When you no longer play scenarios of Jesus mild,
Where wise men follow a star from heaven?

Or does it end when from school you graduate,
As about your life venture you go,
Setting out to find your own special fate?
Did you forget Jesus Christ found in that manger low?

When you found your mate,
What did he hold fast within his heart?
Was it filled with world challenges and hate
Or glad tidings heard from bells in the mart?

Were your years without children devoid of thoughts above,
Filled with seeking the world's pleasures?
Was there no room for the peace and love,
Which Jesus Christ brought in overflowing measures?

When you had children was a cycle complete?
Did you return to seek the joys of childhood,
Not knowing what you would meet?
Could you lead them to find the same Babe, true and good?

Would the Jesus who invited the children
To come and be near Him as He taught,
Not want you as an adult to be near always,
To seek the tidings of love, comfort, and peace that He brought?

You can invite Him to come into your heart,
To hold Him there the whole year through.
Then the entire year may become like Christmas,
Filled with love, peace, and good will.

Teaching Childern Truths About Jesus

. . . Through Fun and Play.
Let His Love Shine On Others
Through My Children And Me.
He Is Our Hope

Is Christmas Only For Children?

Devotions for Day 1

"Train up a child in the way he should go, and when he is old he will not depart from it."

Proverbs 22:6

The Bible makes it plain that if Christmas, the birth of Jesus Christ, our Savior, and the good news that He brought to earth are important to us as a child, they will more likely be important to us when we are older. But those who are raised and remain in the church and think their attendance and membership are ways to salvation will have a huge surprise. Jesus tells us, "Strive to enter by the narrow door; for many, I tell you, will seek to enter and will not be able" (Luke 13:24).

If we try to come to Jesus because of our good works, we will be rejected. That we were once children of God does not make us always and automatically children of God. Jesus makes plain the importance that little children come to Him to learn about His gospel and teachings. "Let the children come to me, and do not hinder them; for to such belongs the kingdom of heaven" (Matthew 19:14). When we become Christians, we enter into individual relationships with our Lord. Trust, acceptance, and love are needed for salvation in Jesus Christ, our Savior, whether as children or adults and whether we have been in the church a short time or all our lives. Ephesians 2:8-9 states "For by grace you have been saved through faith; and this is not your own doing, it is the gift of God—not because of works, least any man should boast." Let's look for ways to make Christmas meaningful for our teens and young adults by giving them an active part in our celebrations.

Prayer:

Dear Lord, we pray for our adolescents and young adults as they are going through many new experiences that expose them to so many new and different ideas. We ask that you will keep them close to you and to people who are committed to you. Give them the courage to stand up for you in their daily lives. Amen.

Is Christmas Only For Children?

Devotions for Day 2

"So, because you are lukewarm, and neither cold nor hot, I will spew you out of my mouth."

Revelation 3:16

There comes a time in the lives of many young people when they feel they have grown out of the teachings of their childhood, especially those of Christmas. It is like growing out of your clothes when the smaller size no longer fits. Some become too sophisticated, and proud to talk about Jesus. Many either stop attending church or become lukewarm Christians. In the above verse, Jesus expresses His displeasure with this behavior by saying he would spit them out. When teenagers and young adults are searching to find their careers and choose their mates, they often have minimal or no contact with the Lord. Our divorce rate has risen to fifty percent or more. What do you think has contributed to so many divorces?

In Genesis, we learn that Abraham lived around the Canaanites, who worshipped many idols. So Abraham sent a servant back to Abraham's own people to get a wife for his son, who believed in the one true God. Acting out of strong faith and obedience to God, Abraham commanded his servant, "he will send his angel before you, and you shall take a wife for my son from there" (Genesis 24:7). Is there a lesson to be learned here about the way a Christian should go about choosing a mate? Help us find ways to involve our teens and those home from college in ways that make them feel wanted and needed in service.

Prayer:

Lord, we want so much for our young people to grow up knowing you in their lives. We ask that you will help us be better examples and take more time to bring the teens in our lives to you so that they better understand your ways and teachings. Amen.

Is Christmas Only For Children?

Devotions for Day 3

"Fathers, do not provoke your children, lest they become discouraged."

Colossians 3:21

When our children are no longer in the Christmas events at church, how are we involving our children in our homes to honor Jesus and give thanks for His perfect gift? Some children will find ways on their own to stay involved but not the majority. In Colossians, Paul tells us not to discourage our children. The Webster Lexicon Dictionary (1989) defines *discouraged* to mean to feel disheartened and hopeless.

In Colossians, the emphasis is on the personal relationship we have with Christ. False teachings were invading their church. We are instructed to believe, obey, love, and rejoice only in the promises of Christ. Just as a church can insist on such strict obedience to a requirement that the importance of Jesus is reduced, likewise, parents can make their children resentful and rebellious by the way they discipline. It is vital that parents help their teens use judgment and problem solving for themselves. Following their peers often leads to drugs, alcohol, and acts of stealing. If you intimidate and disrespect your neighbor how will your child behave in the same situation? How can children contribute to the church or help out at home? An attitude of respect and kindness is essential.

It takes time to nurture. Ephesians 6:4 says, "Fathers, do not provoke your children to anger, but bring them up in the discipline and instruction of the Lord." Perhaps parent groups may use this book to discuss making Christmas more meaningful for teens and young adults.

Prayer:

Dear Lord, we bring before you all the teen-agers of our country. They are our hope that our country will continue to be a Christian nation. Help us nurture them in your admonitions and see their needs. Give us patience and open our eyes to see your guidance. Amen

Is Christmas Only For Children?

Devotions for Day 4

[Jesus] taught, "Let the children come to me, do not hinder them; for to such belongs the kingdom of God. Truly, I say to you, whoever does not receive the kingdom of God like a child shall not enter it."

Mark 10:14-15

One of the greatest stories children learn at Christmas is how much God loved them when he sent his Son, Jesus, as a baby to this earth. They learn to believe and know in their hearts that they are loved and that Jesus wants them to be part of His family. In Mark, Jesus taught that to be saved, we first must admit our sinful nature and our need for His mercy. So when the disciples didn't want to bother with children, He said "unless you turn and become like children, you will never enter the kingdom of heaven" (Matthew 18:3). He taught that self-righteous and pompous people are not in heaven; those in heaven have a simple faith like children. Children are loving, trusting, and teachable.

Some folks feel that children are innocent and don't need baptism. Ever watched a toddler covet his sibling's toys? Teenagers become independent and frequently think they don't need God or parents. They may say they are too old for Christmas or church activities. But we are aware of the evil around them, which they deny or minimize, and we do not throw them out to sink or swim. They need to be taught with patience and understanding to handle problems, such as thinking they are too old or experiencing conflicts in relationships, prejudice, and hatred. Christian teachers and parents help them solve, cope, and turn these problems into something good in their lives.

Prayer:

Dear Lord, help us see the problems that our teenagers are having, give us patience to teach and nurture them according to your word. Help us to let them know we love them and help us teach them how much you love them. This we ask in Jesus' name. Amen.

Is Christmas Only For Children

Devotions for day 5

"And how from childhood you have been acquainted with the sacred writings which are able to instruct you for salvation through faith in Jesus Christ."

2 Timothy 3:15

One of the biblical children that we learn about is Timothy. His upbringing is not different in many ways from what children living today experience. How did his parents succeed in raising a Christian youth in such difficult times? Timothy, born in Lustra, was from a mixed marriage that was condemned by strict Jewish civil law. His father was a Greek Gentile. We don't know what happened to his dad, but his religious schooling was left to his mother, Eunice. He was also taught by his grandmother, Lois. Likewise, today more and more grandparents step in to help raise their grandchildren.

All Christian parents could model after Eunice and Lois. Truths from God's word were taught. They took him to religious meetings held after Paul's second missionary journey, and they instructed him in communication with God through prayer. Each Christmas, parents have many opportunities to instruct their children and help them grow in their faith.

Paul had met Timothy when he was quite young. "I am reminded of your sincere faith, a faith that dwelt first in your grandmother Lois and your mother Eunice and now, I am sure, dwells in you" (2 Timothy 1:5). The Holy Spirit began and maintained this sincere faith. Even when Timothy was a young lad, Paul wanted to work with him, and when Timothy was older, he joined Paul in spreading the gospel.

Prayer:

Help us, O Lord, to lead all our children to you so that through the Holy Spirit they will continue to live Christian lives in sincere faith for you. Amen.

Is Christmas Only For Children?

Devotions for Day 6

"Be glad, for this your brother was dead, and is alive; he was lost, and is found".

Luke 15:32

As children grow up, they leave home for many reasons. Some leave behind the truths taught at Christmas, and others continue in a sincere faith that has grown over the years. Some leave in a huff, and others with their parents' blessings. But all children need opportunities to grow, forgiveness when they fail, and more chances to succeed. Are you there for your children if they need you? Do you bring them before the Lord in prayer?

Parents who have a close relationship with their children seem to intuitively be aware of when their children are having problems coping with life. Our relationship with Jesus is very much the same. He knows all about us, our strengths, weaknesses, and thoughts. We can't hide anything from Him. How do we feel when we are caught doing something we were taught not to do? Normally, we feel guilty. If we come to our senses, we return to the trust and belief we had as children. Having sincere faith in Jesus, we ask forgiveness. Renewed in spirit, children may ask forgiveness of their earthly parents too. Are there not daily situations where parents should bring their concerns about their children before God in prayer? Are there times parents should ask their children for forgiveness?

In the parable of the Prodigal son, (Luke 15:11-32), there is a father who truly had compassion and love for both sons: the prodigal son who asked for forgiveness and the one remaining at home who was angry and jealous. Jesus wants us, children and adults, to be near Him and to seek the love, forgiveness, and peace He brought.

Prayer:

Lord, you work through the Holy Spirit to answer our prayers long before we know to ask for your help in life's situations. Thank you for your love, peace, and forgiveness. Amen.

Spiritual Readings And Devotions

"Jesus"

There are those in these years who still hate Him.
They will do anything they can to stop your faith.
They plot and plan destruction of property and limb
And will persecute Christians and their mates.

They boldly declare the Bible is a fraud
And list why they think that is so,
Saying any book that brings God glory and laud
Must have been written by lunatics below.

They say the winners are the fittest,
Even if they lie, steal, and persecute.
They make fun of the birth of Jesus, the Son of the Highest,
Not believing the news brought by an angel's voice and flute.

They will do what they can to bring life's raging destruction and ripples,
Including demolishing the pictures and books that we love.
They are quick to call believers naïve and simple
And discredit any messages from above.

As in the days of Jesus they believe not
The message of Christmas that was sent.
They continue not to teach their children as tots
To ponder what the angel's messages meant.

But there will be an accounting.
Jesus has promised that this will be so,
And I will be grieved at not finding you there,
In the home that Jesus promised in His heaven of blue.

Written to bring awareness of the harassment and stealing that has occurred and continues to occur in Sacramento, California so that we do not forget that all freedom we have must be won and claimed for each generation. These acts consisted of burning churches, stealing valuable relics, and destruction of property. It also included the stealing of several of my poems. The culprits of these crimes were usually not identified.

Jesus

Devotions for Day 1

"Now the chief priests and the whole *council sought false testimony against Jesus that they might put him to death".*

Matthew 26:59

The scribes and the Pharisees feared that Jesus would replace them, and they had been constantly trying to trap Jesus with questions. These groups were known throughout the nation of Israel for the role they played in their religious functions. They knew the law for all its minute details and demanded strict observances of it. In reality, Jesus found that the hearts of many from these groups were far from His teachings. Jesus became an obstacle they wanted to get rid of, as people were following Him because of His teachings and miracles. The people "glorified God, who had given such authority to men" but the scribes were enraged when Jesus said He could "forgive sins" (Matthew 9:6, 8).

Today, one will find the same types of events occurring, and people continue to deal with the same prejudices against Christianity. These people will report anything, often lying or misrepresenting the truth. They cause much disunity in the church with their accusations about Jesus. Christmas often becomes a time when our beliefs are challenged. What stand will you take and will you seek Jesus for your answers?

Prayer:

We thank you Lord, for giving us the steadfast presence of Jesus's love in our lives. We ask that the Holy Spirit deepen our faith in Jesus Christ. When Satan presents falsehoods and new thinking to confuse us, we ask for your help to remain firmly in your word and love, which never change. Let us give thanks for the religious freedoms we have this Christmas and practice these freedoms through the whole year. Amen.

Jesus

Devotions for Day 2

"So the chief priests and the Pharisees gathered the council, and said, "What are we to do? For this man performs many signs. If we let him go on thus, everyone will believe in him, and the Romans will come and destroy both our holy place and our nation.""

John 11:47-48

Jesus raised Martha and Mary's brother, Lazarus, from the dead. This was the third person He had raised from the dead. In the Bible, the number three is associated with perfection and mystery, as in the Trinity. It may represent the fact that Jesus's ministry was nearing completion. In a month, he too would die. Soon after Lazarus's resurrection, the Sanhedrin, chief priests, and Pharisees agreed that they should kill Jesus. The New Lexicon Webster's Dictionary (1989) defines the *Sanhedrin* as the Jewish Supreme council (court of justice) consisting of seventy one priests, scribes, and elders.

These last events must have been confusing times for followers, as their former beliefs were challenged. As secular Christmas stories and activities invade our lives, our focus on Jesus can also be lost. When we are restored as God's children in baptism, we enter a strong bond that connects us forever to Jesus as He walks with us. The Holy Spirit works to restore us again if we become lost. When Peter rebuked Jesus for foretelling of His persecution and death, Jesus responded to Peter, "Get behind me, Satan! You are a hindrance to me; for you are not on the side of God, but of men" (Matthew 16:23). Each Christmas help us find ways to gently teach our children to remain humbly in your service.

Prayer:

Help us, dear Lord, to grow in Christ and wisdom so that we might know how to handle temptations from Satan as these occur in our lives and in our nation. Make us aware, and may our faith be strong as we seek your will for our lives. Amen.

Jesus

Devotions for Day 3

"And when they had assembled with the elders and taken counsel, they gave a sum of money to the soldiers and said, "Tell people, 'His disciples came by night and stole him away while we were asleep.""

Matthew 28:12-13

The Pharisees and high priests became afraid the disciples would come and steal the body of Jesus. They went to Pilate, who told them, "You have a guard of soldiers; go, make it as secure as you can" (Matthew 27:65). So, they sealed the stone, putting guards at the sepulcher. Matthew 28:1-6 tells us how God intervened in their plans. Just as at the birth of Jesus, God again used angels as His messengers. The angel of the Lord came in a great earthquake, rolled the stone away, caused the soldiers to fell to the ground, and was there when the two women came at dawn to tell them Jesus has risen.

The guards rushed to report these events to the Sanhedrin. The Bible does not tell us if these Pharisees and high priests knew about the Christmas story and the peace, love and joy Jesus had brought. Their only thought was that they would loose their jobs if the people followed Jesus. The guards were given large sums of money to lie and tell the people that the disciples had come during the night and stole the body as they slept. Matthew 28:15 says, "So they took the money and did as they were directed; and this story has been spread among the Jews to this day."

Prayer:

O Lord, when persecution comes make us strong and obedient to do your will. Show us your way, the truth, and the light. We ask for your help finding ways that make Christmas meaningful and a joyous season. Amen.

Jesus

Devotions for Day 4

"For I am the least of the apostles, unfit to be called an apostle, because I persecuted the church of God."

I Corinthians 15:9

Paul was from a Jewish, Greek, and Roman background. He was a Pharisee and appeared to be a member of the Sanhedrin; at this time, he was called Saul. He came from Tarsus to Jerusalem, where he became involved in persecuting the church and where he attended the stoning of Stephen.

Stephen was appointed as one of the seven deacons who spent time telling the story of Jesus to the multitudes of visitors to Jerusalem. Huge numbers of believers were gained from their teachings. So, the Jews made up charges against Stephen, saying "We have heard him speak blasphemous words against Moses and God" (Acts 6:11). Stephen was brought before the Sanhedrin, where he became the first Christian martyr.

At Christmas, we celebrate the birth of Jesus as a baby. It is here and at the crucifixion that we have opportunities to witness the great love that Jesus had for all humankind. The gospel was new to Saul, but in Jerusalem he witnessed those living firmly for Christ, knowing the love that Jesus had for us. Saul was being made ready to be receptive to the vision he was to behold. Paul's (Saul) direction was soon reversed and he did more to establish Christianity in the known world than any man except Jesus. Focusing on Jesus may help us do the tasks given us, when struggling with temptations at Christmas.

Prayer:

We ask for your guidance and strength in our own daily struggles. Help us to be there in fellowship with other Christians when our help is needed. When persecutions against Christians occurs help us stand up for Jesus and do our part to witness for Him. Amen.

Jesus

Devotions for Day 5

"For thou, O Lord, art good and forgiving, abounding in steadfast love to all who call on thee."

Psalms 86:5

Saul was hard-pressed to bring the Jewish Christian into compliance with the strict Jewish civil law. Many were imprisoned, beaten, and put to death. Saul was on his way to Damascus when he had a vision of Jesus. According to Acts 9:4, Saul heard the voice of Jesus from heaven, "Saul, Saul, why do you persecute me?" After this, Saul was sightless for three days until the Lord appeared to Ananias, a servant, and sent him to Saul to restore his sight, baptize him, and rename him Paul. Ananias was afraid of Saul but the Lord said, "Go, for he is a chosen instrument of mine to carry my name before the Gentiles and kings and sons of Israel" (Acts 9:15).

Just like the Christmas message brought to earth by Jesus, the story of Paul is part of God's plan for salvation to all people. God was preparing Paul for his missionary work. It is incomprehensible for a non-believer, without faith, to understand God's plan, and the faithless ridicule and joke about it. After his vision, Paul worked as diligently and passionately for the Lord's church as he had in persecuting it. Jesus does indeed change hearts, and Paul proclaimed the good news of great joy to all people; Jews, and Gentiles, the same good news that the angels had brought to the shepherds. Let us share God's plan in simple faith with our children at Christmas. We can also help them understand by reading the poems and devotions with them.

Prayer:

Help us to be aware of when persecution occurs so that we stop it. Open all hearts to your word Lord, that we may receive forgiveness of sins by grace through faith in Jesus. Amen.

Jesus

Devotions for Day 6

"If they persecuted me, they will persecute you; if they kept my word, they will keep yours also."

John 15:20

God's plan for baby Jesus, whose birth we celebrate each Christmas continues to be made clear to those concerned. But we cannot see as God sees. Mary and Joseph took Jesus to the temple in Jerusalem for His purification rites. At the temple was a man called Simeon, who had a vision that he would not die until he saw the Messiah. In Luke 2:35 he told Mary, "(and a sword will pierce through your own soul also)." He was prophesying how Mary would feel when Jesus would be persecuted and crucified for the sins of all people.

United States was settled by people who came here to end the persecution they were experiencing because of their beliefs. We are now living in times when those who don't believe, speak out stronger than those who do believe in Jesus. They base equality on denying prayer to our school children while on school grounds, trying to remove "In God We Trust" from our coins, and stopping prayer in our higher courts. They do this all in the name of freedom so as not to offend any religion. How crafty Satan works to cloud our minds. But 2 Timothy 2:12 states, "if we deny him, he also will deny us". The Israelites of the Old Testament had to deal with neighbors who practiced pagan religions. How well did that all turn out for them when they were not obedient to God? Honoring Jesus at Christmas is a necessity for my spiritual growth and freedom of religion. What will or has made Christmas meaningful for you and your family? Perhaps you will want to do more of the same.

Prayer:

Forgive us, Lord, if we too interfere with your work to bring the good news of the gospel to all nations. Help us to seek your will through prayer and meditation with you. Amen.

Spiritual Readings And Devotions

"The Spirit of Christmas"

Santa comes in different statures, you reassure,

He's not only fat with cheeks alit

But is a slender rail in a red suit and fur,

And with the children, he is a definite hit.

So, where did he come from,

And why is Santa so much fun?

Did he make a deal with the toy maker who builds the drums,

Or is the spirit of Christmas meant for everyone?

Did someone invent him to help make a living,

And is there a lesson to be taught?

Or is there more behind the story of giving,

The difference between goodness and evil to be fought?

Where did your child learn about Santa?

Or do you care what they think?

Are the children all the same from Montreal to Atlanta,

And can he interlink all countries with a wink?

What does your heart tell you about Christmas,

Of which jolly old Saint Nicholas is a part?

As there is a connection for an isthmus,

Does he depend upon a parent to be his counterpart?

I choose to believe in the spirit of Christmas,
When the birth of the babe Jesus brought so much joy.
In my book Santa Claus is a definite hit.
Like Jesus giving love so freely Santa gives his gifts of toys.

Father Christmas, Santa Claus,
Known for his jolly laughter,
Sintar Klaus, Saint Nicholas,
And his smile of contentment the night after.

The Spirit of Christmas

Devotions for Day 1

"He who did not spare his own Son but gave him up for us all, will he not also give us all things with him"?

Romans 8:32

The spirit of Christmas is symbolic of giving. We have one of the best gifts we could ever receive in Jesus Christ, our Savior, who was born on Christmas. He died so that our sins can be forgiven and we can learn about a new life in Christ. We forget, but the Holy Spirit never forgets and is making unceasing intercessions for us in this new life. Through prayer, we are assured that everything that happens will work together for our good. As our trust grows in Christ, we learn that there is no power that can stop us from belonging to Jesus when we humbly seek Him.

The concept of our Santa Claus came from a real bishop called Saint Nicholas who took gifts to the needy. A day in December was set aside for celebrating a feast in his honor where good children were remembered with gifts. So the idea of Santa Claus includes the concept of giving and reinforces the concepts of goodness and obedience. However, here the giving of gifts comes from an earthly father. The idea of Santa Claus allows for the occasion when gifts can be given by an elderly, kind man. If a child receives good gifts from an earthly father, is it not more likely that they can believe that the heavenly Father sent a gift to them on Christmas, that of Jesus Christ, our Savior?

Prayer:

Father in heaven, may our acts of giving benefit both us and the receiver. Help us to be aware and responsive to the needs of children. Let us discipline them when it is needed and love them always. May our acts of giving, bear fruits for a life in Christ. Amen

The Spirit of Christmas

Devotions for Day 2

"If you then, who are evil, know how to give good gifts to your children, how much more will your Father who is in heaven give good things to those who ask him!"

Matthew 7:11

There is a large variety of different stories about Christmas. I recently heard one where the celebration of the block consisted of neighborhood house lighting contests and of Christmas Eve parties or "bashes," as they were called. With the wrong emphasis, many people experience the negatives of Christmas. For example, there are the unwanted presents, the outrageous cost for liquid, food, and lightings, and the jealousy and resentment of neighbors. And don't forget the arguments.

In many of these stories Jesus is not mentioned. Do people visiting the United States leave knowing how important Jesus is to us? If you don't know Jesus and don't celebrate His birth, Christmas indeed becomes meaningless.

Can you help your child better understand the concept of giving? We talk about the gift of the birth of Jesus, and the spirit of Christmas becomes alive with meaning in our hearts, as we remember that the Messiah who loves us so much had come on this day. Through Santa Claus, all children, both rich and poor, receive gifts from their earthly fathers and mothers, given simply because someone loved them. The gift maybe anticipated and upon receiving it there is much joy. Likewise, it is our job to teach our children to have as much joy in giving as in receiving.

Prayer:

O Lord, we are truly blessed by the choice of your gift to us. Let us chose as wisely for our children. Help us teach them about the Spirit of Christmas. Amen.

The Spirit of Christmas

Devotions for Day 3

"Remembering the words of the Lord Jesus, how he said, 'It is more blessed to give then to receive.'"

Acts 20:35

The true spirit of Christmas is in giving. But our giving in not perfect and always seems to be of a selfish nature. God's perfect gift was given to us in the baby Jesus. Who would have thought that God's blessing would come as a baby? Just as the Jews did not expect their salvation to come as a baby, do we see our blessings for what they are? On a daily basis, it seems to me that we take most blessings for granted.

Our children need to be taught to give and this giving may be different for each person. For example, we learn through Bible stories. Our parents help us become ready to hear about how much Jesus loved us and the wonderful gifts we receive through the Holy Spirit. Each one of us may serve the Lord according to the gift he was given.

We can also learn by hearing of Santa Claus's acts of giving. Because of the giving of gifts by Santa, some may believe that someone other than our parents can love us. Peter, likewise, taught new Christians how to receive guidance and strength from God's word. In 1 Peter 2: 2-3, we were taught "Like newborn babes, long for the pure spiritual milk, that by it you may grow up to salvation; for you have tasted the kindness of the Lord." Growing stronger in faith and grace is a process, and we will repeatedly need the simple milk of God's word to accomplish this. As we grow in our relationship with Jesus, the Holy Spirit helps us understand our obligations to God that we may become a blessing to others. What spiritual goals have you set for yourself this Christmas?

Prayer:

Dear Lord, help us grow in understanding and faith. Thank you for your blessing that all good things through you may be turned into blessings for others. Amen.

The Spirit of Christmas

Devotions for Day 4

"For God loves a cheerful giver."

2 Corinthians 9:7

Jesus used all manner of unlikely people to help Him spread His gospel. God's church is made up of a tattered body of believers who are sinners, unwanted, and outcasts. So would not Jesus use a character like Santa Claus to bring all people the spirit of Christmas, especially those who are very young Christians and are learning the basic concepts of giving?

In reality, Santa can be used for the power of goodness or the power of evil, just like most things in this world. How He is used in your life depends upon you. In 2 Corinthians 9:1-15, Paul is giving instructions for the churches of Macedonia, Achaia, and Galatia to give an offering of support to the church in Jerusalem. They were taught by Paul to give generously, not grudgingly. When we walk with God in total commitment, it results in generous, joyous service. Then, indeed, we experience the spirit of Christmas in our hearts. The Bible tells us that David was a man after God's own heart. Acts 13:23 says, "Of this man's posterity God has brought to Israel a Savior, Jesus, as he promised." When our hearts are right with God, anything is possible.

Prayer:

Dear Lord, help us see your will for our lives, and give to others in joyous service to you. Give us the strength and knowledge to teach our children the concepts of giving that comes from the heart that loves you, according to your will. Amen.

The Spirit of Christmas

Devotions for Day 5

"'This people honors me with their lips, but their heart is far from me; in vain do they worship me, teaching as doctrines the precepts of men.'"

Matthew 15:8-9

Christian living may consist of attending church on Sunday, keeping the ten commandments, and giving tithes. But the rest of the week, many live as if they have never heard of Jesus. Jesus was troubled about this in the people of His time too. They would not let Jesus save a dying man on the Sabbath because of their strict observances. Today, many people attend church activities on Christmas and then don't go to church for months or participate in religious activities during the week. Are these people receiving the spirit of Christmas, the joy of living, and the inner peace that Jesus wishes for all of us?

We know that Satan can use times of stress, which occurs at Christmas, to make us question, doubt, and disbelieve. Also, some people object to a belief in Santa Claus. Santa has qualities that we want to instill in our children, such as generosity, cheerfulness, and concern for all, rich or poor. It is up to us, as parents and teachers, to train our children in the true spirit of Christmas. Thus, in spite of the hustle and bustle of the season, Jesus does not get lost from our thoughts, because we remember Him as the most important gift given by God. When we seek Him at Christmas, the Holy Spirit guides and directs us so that Jesus remains the focus. What Jesus wants most is for us to return one of the gifts He has given. Jesus wants us to love Him and He wants our hearts to belong to Him. This Christmas, take time to discuss with your children how they can show they love Jesus

Prayer:

Dear Lord, we bring all children before you in prayer. Help us, through the Holy Spirit, to return your love and to teach our children about you. We love you and want to give our hearts to you . . . Amen.

The Spirit of Christmas

Devotions for Day 6

"And I am sure that he who began a good work in you will bring it to completion at the day of Jesus Christ."

Philippians 1:6

Each of us has a Christmas focus that is important to us. Is this not demonstrated by what we talk about on Christmas Eve? Let's make it something worth remembering. If we turn to the Bible, we see Jesus, who came as God's word to us. Through Jesus, we see in God's heart and hear His message to us. We find His everlasting love that never stops.

Christmas is when God gave us His marvelous, wonderful gift. Do we bring our children to worship Him at this time? Secular Christmastime activities include bringing gifts to our very young children from Santa Claus. The essence of the spirit of Christmas is focused on giving. What connection do we make for our children as they grow? Can gift giving be a stepping stone to the true message of Christmas? One question asked is, how can a baby be our guide and our protector? Those who ask this question do not yet understand the love and power that brought Jesus to earth. Isaiah 9:6 tells us that we are strong, as Jesus stands with us as the "Wonderful Counselor, Mighty God, Everlasting Father, Prince of Peace." As parents, one of the best gifts we give is to pray with our children, talk about Jesus, share stories, and spend time with them. God does not always reveal His plans to us for our children. We trust and pray that the Lord will work His purpose through the Holy Spirit in our children. He is the hope of us all.

Prayer:

Dear heavenly Father, help us do our part in bringing our children to you and correcting them when we know they need our help. Help us to place our trust in you, and grant us your peace. This we ask in Jesus's name. Amen

Spiritual Readings And Devotions

"We Are Thankful"

We give thanks for your coming as a gentle shepherd,
For filling us with a food that leaves no hunger.
We are thankful for the Word we heard,
And for your blessings even thought we often be a bungler.

We are thankful that you came to unharden hearts
And brought peace and good will as the angel sing.
Lord, you alone provide for the blessing at our hearths,
And we give thanks that you came as our Savior, our King.

We are thankful that as a babe you came down from above
To deliver us from our sin and world's evils,
Bringing us your wondrous gift of love,
So that we are granted peace inspite of life's upheavals.

We are thankful for the miracle of your birth,
For giving us much needed rest and peace,
And for coming to show us what is true worth;
Only then did sin and selfishness cease.

We are thankful dear Lord, for your gift.
We are thankful that you heard our plea,
Showing us the Way to heal a rift,
And to you we will swiftly flee.

We are Thankful

Devotions for Day 1

"Thanks be to God for his inexpressible gift!"

2 Corinthians 9:15

We have an individual relationship with God through Jesus Christ and are most thankful for the miraculous birth of Jesus, our Savior, for His coming to earth as man and as God. I am thankful for Jesus taking all my sins on Himself that I might be saved, that I might become one of his children again, and I am thankful that He has given me eternal life. These we all have received through the grace of Jesus Christ and not of our own doing.

Personally, I am thankful that I live in a country where I can read the Bible freely and study from it, and I am thankful for everything I have been given. I am thankful that I live at a time when we enjoy so many modern conveniences, such as indoor plumbing, automobiles, and electricity, to name a few. But I am most thankful that God has given me His guidance and care these past years as I struggled to regain my health and restore broken bones. I am thankful for the working of the Holy Spirit in my life, as through Him I have grown in sharing experiences in my Christian life with others. Making a list of why you are thankful may be helpful in your growth as you bring these before the Lord in prayer.

Prayer:

Jesus, I thank you for all your blessings and love. As sinners, we deserve none of these. Thank you for work, health, family, friends, for money to pay the bills, and for everything that we have or will have. We ask that you will continue to give us all these blessings in Jesus's name. Amen

We are Thankful

Devotions for Day 2

"So, whether you eat or drink, or whatever you do, do all to the glory of God."

I Corinthians 10:31

At Christmas we are especially thankful for the gift we received so many years ago: God's son, Jesus Christ. Many of our holiday celebrations include eating and drinking. If we do not do this in moderation, we may offend others. Eating and drinking can become "a stumbling block" for some people (Romans 14:13-21). An example might be drinking to intoxication and then driving drunk. As Christians, we are not to use food and drink for abuse or if it injures another, but for enjoyment with each other as we honor and thank God for His blessings. This would be especially true at Christmas as we share meals where we are glorifying our heavenly Father for His generous and precious gifts given so freely for us.

We should all give thanks and praise the Lord for His help and mercy all year long, not just at Christmas. We give honor to God Almighty as we praise His glorious name. We tell Him that we love Him, that we thank Him for His gifts, and for all the other things in our lives that He has provided over the years. We also find opportunities to teach our children what pleases Jesus and to explain that each child is a precious gift from God entrusted in our care.

Prayer:

Almighty God, you have provided so much for me over the years and I bring all of these things before you with a thankful heart (make a list of things that you are thankful for). As I celebrate the birth of your Son, Jesus Christ, let me use food, drink, and my life in a manner that honors you. Praise be to God. Amen.

We are Thankful

Devotions for Day 3

"And you will say in that day: "Give thanks to the Lord, call upon his name; make known his deeds among the nations, proclaim that his name is exalted.""

Isaiah 12:4

My life would be very different, I am sure, if Jesus Christ had not come to this earth for me and for you so many years ago. After Jesus came, the practice of sacrifices was stopped. Jesus was the ultimate sacrifice! And He shows His love and mercy to me by giving me the peace and joy He brought that first Christmas night. All we have to do is ask, and these gifts are granted. At Christmas we thank God for all He has given us. We should not only do this at Christmas but continue the practice of thanking Him day after day.

We are instructed to let all nations know what He has done for us. As an individual, I talk to my family, neighbors, friends, and acquaintances about what Jesus has done in my life and how important He has been to me. After starting to share with others more, I truly became aware of the many ways He intercedes in my life. After sharing, I no longer take for granted most of what has happened in my life.

Prayer:

We praise you Lord Jesus, for all the wonderful changes you brought to this earth. Through your teachings we learned to have more compassion for our fellow human beings. Help us to be strong, obedient, and courageous in our spreading of your word as you instructed us, so that others may know of you as their Savior. This we ask in Jesus's name. Amen.

We are Thankful

Devotions for Day 4

"Addressing one another in psalms and hymns and spiritual songs, singing and making melody to the Lord with all your heart, always and for everything giving thanks in the name of our Lord Jesus Christ to God the Father."

Ephesians 5:19-20

Christmas is a time when we honor and give thanks for the miracle of Jesus's birth and music is one way we can give thanks for the special gifts we received. There are many Christmas hymns that retell the story of His birth and of the limitless blessings of joy, love, and peace brought to each of us by this gentle shepherd. Participating in Christmas music is like putting on the armor of God. Making music with all our hearts is stimulating, creative, inspiring, glorifying, uplifting, and can be very powerful.

Reviewing the history of the early church shows us how much of Paul's teaching concentrated on the differences between Christian life and heathen worship, with music occurring in both. His teachings are just as relevant for today. Christmas music is a religious tool that is used to honor, to grow stronger against the powers of this earth, and to give thanks. Riotous, drunken sprees, which occurred as part of the heathen ceremonies, used music to stir up the people so they would become uninhibited and give in to natural temptations and sexual orgies. Christian singing is to make us more aware of our obligations, to express love, and to honor the Lord. It can also restore joy, give us peace in our daily worship, and provide us with encouragement for witnessing for Jesus. Christmas concerts, whether we listen or participate, may help make the season more meaningful.

Prayer:

Lord, we give thanks for everything you have given us so freely. We thank you for this gift of Jesus Christ, whom you sent to restore us as your children. Accept our gratitude. Show us ways to use music for your honor and your glory. Amen.

We are Thankful

Devotions for Day 5

[Jesus] said, "Were not ten cleansed? Where are the nine? Was no one found to return and give praise to God except this foreigner?"

Luke 17:17-18

This story about the ten lepers shows, without a doubt, what Jesus wants from us: . . . our love, praise, and thanks. According to Luke, there were ten lepers standing at a distance from the path that Jesus and His disciples were traveling on. They called to Jesus saying, "Jesus, Master, have mercy on us" (Luke 17:13). Jesus instructed them to show themselves to the priests which was an act of obedience and when one of the lepers saw he was healed, he returned to praise and thank Jesus (Luke 17:14-16). Jesus told the healed leper, "Rise and go your way; your faith has made you well" (Luke 17:19). How often do we, as the nine lepers who did not return, forget to give Jesus our praise and thanks?

Forgetfulness and thoughtlessness are common reasons for not giving thanks to God for all our blessings. This is part of our human nature. But when we give thanks, it does please God. It also adds joy to our lives, as it lifts the spirit, heart, and mind. We fail to be grateful so often, but may these devotions be used this Christmas to remind us to give thanks often in whatever way the Holy Spirit leads. Isaiah tells us to give ear to God's teaching, for if we do not, He may not hear our prayers (1:10, 15).

Prayer:

Dear heavenly Father, help us to always thank you daily for your many blessings, be obedient to your word, and acknowledge you as our Lord and Savior every day. Amen

We are Thankful

Devotions for Day 6

"For although they knew God they did not honor him as God or give thanks to him, but they become futile in their thinking and their senseless minds were darkened." . . . . *"Therefore, God gave them up to the lusts of their hearts to impurity, to the dishonoring of their bodies among themselves."*

Romans 1:21, 24

Paul speaks about the sinfulness of all humankind in this chapter. We are all guilty of one or more of the sins Paul lists in the following verses, and we need God's forgiveness. Paul taught that what was important was not whether we were Jewish or Gentile but what was in our hearts. As the gospel spread, this became an important part of his teachings, as some of the Jewish people argued about customs, demanding that everyone take part or they could not belong to the church. But this was a truth that God had long tried to teach the Israelites. In the Old Testament the Lord spoke to Samuel saying, "for the Lord sees not as man sees; man looks on the outward appearance, but the Lord looks on the heart" (1 Samuel 16:7).

Paul tells us very directly and up front that God will abandon us if we persist in this neglect of our worship by not giving thanks. In Romans, Paul sends an explanation of the gospel to Rome. Our forgiveness is based on the mercy of Christ: His dying for our sins, His resurrection, and His overcoming Satan. His mercy endures forever. Just as the early church needed to be taught by Paul, we need to be taught and then teach our children to give thanks and honor Jesus Christ. Let this be a priority this Christmas.

Prayer:

Jesus, help us to be obedient to your commandments. Show us ways to gently correct our children and other Christians as they slip into sinful ways that bring you displeasure. Let us remember to daily give thanks for the blessings you bestow on us. Amen.

Spiritual Readings And Devotions

"My Miracle"

Thank you Lord Jesus, for the love you have given me.
Thank you for the strength you give.
Thank you for the mercy you have shown me,
That a fuller life, I might live.

Thank you for answering my prayers that were given.
Thank you for the help that arrived.
Thank you for everything for which I have been forgiven
And that through your mercy I survived.

Thank you for the comfort granted.
Thank you for the relief of pain.
Thank you for the healing which was wanted,
And that others may in Christ know gain.

Thank you for giving me renewed hope.
Thank you for the courage to drive.
Thank you for guarding against shadows so I can cope,
And that according to your plan, in Christ I am alive.

Thank you for bringing me through my time of doubting.
Thank you for restoring my limb.
Thank you for those who were so giving,
And for bringing into my life those who are committed to Him.

Thank you for helping me experience Christ's love.
Thank you for showing me how high and deep it is.
Thank you for the blessings that come from above.
With wonder and awe I give thanks for all miracles, which are His.

This poem came from my heart in humble gratitude for God's help in restoring my fractured leg and for the many miracles of 9/11 that occurred. My leg did not heal perfectly but I can walk and I give thanks to God for His healing and mercy.

Walking is now a blessing for me and although I still have complications I give thanks from a grateful heart for the healing God has given.

My Miracle

Devotions for Day 1

"Let us run with perseverance the race that is set before us."

Hebrews 12:1

Don't give up. This phrase has been put to music, spoken by parents to their children, and offered encouragingly by teachers to their students. It has also been used in times of crisis by leaders of countries. For a miracle to happen in our lives, we require a lot of faith, trust, and prayers. We also need patience and staying power. Events that require a miracle may be injury and illness, forgiving, learning complicated things, avoiding abuse and temptations, and dealing with people who don't care if they constantly break God's commandments on how to live. Sometimes miracles require the planning and assistance of special people. This was true of my miracle of better health.

A life that is inspiring, exciting, satisfying, and lived for Jesus does not come without struggles. Christmas is a time of inspiration, and we are encouraged to keep our eyes on Jesus. The New Lexicon Webster's Dictionary (1989) defines *inspiration* as "divine influence, seen as the working of the Holy Spirit in the human soul, . . . a supernatural prompting." Do our Christmas activities allow time and space for inspiration? In families where singing is enjoyed, hymns such as "Living for Jesus" or any of the Christmas carols may be a source of inspiration and lift up our spirits. Learning a Christmas carol in a foreign language that is part of our heritage can make singing more meaningful.

Prayer:

God, give us patience and help us reach out for other believers, sharing our burdens, and prayers for each other. Heal us, Lord, and heal our land. Allow our faith to grow, and let us find in your love how to grow in sharing your word with others. Amen.

My Miracle

Devotions for Day 2

"But they who wait for the Lord shall renew their strength, they shall mount up with wings like eagles, they shall run and not be weary, they shall walk and not faint."

Isaiah 40:31

God wants us to be persistent. But what if we are trying to live as Jesus has taught us? It is discouraging to keep repeating the same sins for which Jesus has just forgiven us. Paul said, "For I do not do what I want, but I do that very thing I hate" (Romans 7:15). Will Jesus keep forgiving our sins? I receive mercy from Jesus and not just one day, but every day of my life. We are aware of some sins, but there are others that we are not aware of. We ask Jesus to forgive all our sins, always. If we love Jesus, we will make that effort to overcome our sinning ways. Miracles occur when we are receptive "to the gift of God's grace which was given me by the working of his power" (Ephesians 3:7).

When some people think of Christmas, they think of snow. Snow symbolizes purity. Isaiah 1:18 says, "Though your sins are like scarlet, they shall be as white as snow." This baby Jesus whose birth we are celebrating came to earth so that each day when we get up we start the day knowing God offered forgiveness in Christ. We go to sleep each night asking for forgiveness of our sins, that Jesus will make us white as snow and give us the strength each day to fly free as eagles for Him. What do you do to stay in touch with Jesus every day? Christmas may be a stressful time, so set your priorities and make daily time for prayer and worship.

Prayer:

Jesus, thank you for the miracles that have occurred in our lives and for daily forgiveness of all our sins. Thank you for bringing us through times of doubting, for the renewed hope, and for the comfort you have given us. Amen.

My Miracle

Devotions for Day 3

"Heal me, O Lord, and I shall be healed; save me, and I shall be saved; for thou art my praise."

Jeremiah 17:14

Jeremiah prophesied for forty years, repeatedly telling Judah to repent and God would deliver them from Babylonian captivity but the people would not listen. He gave repeated warnings to Judah to stop idolatry and foretold of the coming destruction of Jerusalem and the temple. Jeremiah also prophesied that a King was coming who would be just and wise. He would be called, "The Lord is our righteousness" (Jeremiah 23:6). Jesus Christ was this King and He took the sins of the whole world on himself when He was crucified. In Christ our sins are not counted against us. Paul said, "For our sake he made him to be sin who knew no sin; so that in him we might become the righteousness of God" (2 Corinthians 5:21). God's righteousness is ours if we have faith in Christ.

The Lord brought a miracle in my life by bringing healing, hope, and comfort. During times of adversity the Holy Spirit works. A person will either listen or grow in faith and understanding or not. "Heal me, O Lord" is a hymn that has a promise from God that you may need in your life. Even thought His love is there all the time, this was special for me as He healed, strengthened, and at the same time challenged that changes be made in one's life. Giving your life to Jesus will indeed make your Christmas special, and Christmas will never be the same if you remain in the Lord.

Prayer:

Lord, Let me be open to your guidance and see opportunities in my life to serve you. Thank you for the love you have shown me. Amen.

My Miracle

Devotions for Day 4

"That according to the riches of his glory he may grant you to be strengthened with might through his Spirit in the inner man, and that Christ may dwell in your hearts through faith; that you, being rooted and grounded in love, may have power to comprehend with all the saints what is the breadth and length and height and depth, and to know the love of Christ which surpasses knowledge, that you may be filled with all the fulness of God."

Ephesians 3:16-19

God reveals His love so many times to us that expecting it can become routine to the point where we stop being thankful. Sometimes God lets things happen that brings us face-to-face with the breadth, length, height, and depth of the love that Jesus has for us. When controversies develop, the Holy Spirit may help us see the evil intentions of Satan's works. God has a way of turning the intentions of people around. Paul experienced one of the best known flip-flops in history when he was converted from a persecutor of Christians to one of Jesus's apostles. Paul listened to Jesus, and a church was established where all humankind had the opportunity to be heirs to God's promises.

Simeon, a devoted Jew, had a revelation that before he died he would see the Messiah. In Luke 2:30-32, when Simeon sees Jesus, he says "for mine eyes have seen thy salvation which thou hast prepared in the presence of all peoples, a light for revelation to the Gentiles, and for glory to thy people Israel." It was God's intent that the gospel was for all people and His plan could not be stopped even when many in the church objected. What can you do, at Christmas to keep freedom of religion alive in your community?

Prayer:

Dear Lord, your love is indeed a miracle in our lives. Thank you for giving us the opportunity to celebrate a Christmas centered on you. As freedoms are threatened in our nation show us how to win freedom of religion back if this be your will and let us find new ways that honor and praise you. Amen

My Miracle

Devotions for Day 5

"Rejoice always, pray constantly, give thanks in all circumstances; for this is the will of God in Christ Jesus for you."

1 Thessalonians 5:16-18

Prayer played a big part in my miracle. Prayer is the way we communicate with Jesus. When we are well, we think we are in charge, but when injured or sick, we know we are not. Then the Lord has our attention. In Joel 2:32, we are told, "And it shall come to pass that all who calls upon the name of the Lord shall be delivered."

There are many books that teach us about prayer. But how do we communicate with God at Christmas-time about what Christmas means to us? We are taught to search the Bible for answers. God was thought to be unapproachable by ordinary people, but Jesus, who was fully man and fully God, came to earth as a baby to teach us about God. God may have sent a baby because ordinary people are not as likely to fear a child. When we seek Jesus, He blots out all sins. How can we pray about our troubles if we think He does not hear us? I have been taught that God always answers prayer but sometimes one is not taking the time to listen for His answer. This can be especially true at Christmas when we are so busy. Prayer is indeed the key to an adventurous, satisfying life. James 5:16 says, "Therefore confess your sins to one another, and pray for one another, that you may be healed. The prayer of a righteous man has great power in its effects." Let your children see you pray and pray with your children!

Prayer:

Lord, we pray for understanding, and guidance in how to apply Jesus's teachings to our own lives. Help us find time for prayer every day and to pray without ceasing. Amen.

My Miracle

Devotions for Day 6

"Therefore take the whole armor of God, that you may be able to withstand in the evil day, and having done all, to stand."

Ephesians 6:13

Many in the young church of Ephesus had practiced pagan beliefs before becoming Christians. Pagan temples, where these sins were practiced daily, existed all around the area. In verse 12, Paul tells us of the power of the rulers of darkness and that we can struggle against these powers by putting on God's whole armor.

There are six gifts that make up the armor of God. The belt is the truth of God's word. The breastplate is the righteousness of Christ. The shoes are the gospel of peace. The shield stops the arrows of the wicked. The helmet is salvation, and the sword of the spirit is the word of God. We can only win against Satan by using the sword. Hebrews 4:12 says, "For the word of God is living and active, sharper than any two-edged sword, piercing to the division of soul and spirit, of joints and marrow, and discerning the thoughts and intentions of the heart." My miracle took place when I struggled against evil practices existing in my community. Wearing the armor of God gave me the strength to write and share my Christmas joy, and by sharing I increased my own joy. Let's search for ways to creatively put meaning back into Christmas such as inviting a child to your church activities or visiting a shut in, not to stop loneliness, but to spread the good news, then Jesus works in their lives. Let's make this the most joyous Jesus-focused Christmas ever.

Prayer:

Lord, my prayer is that you will use these spiritual poems and devotions to spread the good news as it is your will. Let each of us use the gifts you gave us to your honor and glory. Help us remember that you are ever present and use the armor of God in our daily struggles. Amen.

Spiritual Readings And Devotions

"Christmas"

Once again it is Christmas,
And I wonder if my poem will rhyme.
And will my message be inspiring
For all the promises it can bring?

It has been a year of healing.
It has been a year of dashed hopes,
Of unfaithfulness at every kneeling,
But strengthening for the one who copes.

Evil in the world is rampant,
Yet Christ is my guide and stay,
And I will manage my part as confidant,
Because my worries through Him are cast away.

The words of hope come to mind:
"Only believe," are the words you will find.
And so it has been a year of testing
To find out if our faith is lasting.

As I bravely face the uncertainties that life can bring,
The words, "All is possible through Jesus Christ," are given,
And to this promise I will cling,
As through Jesus Christ, we are forgiven.

Now we celebrate the birth of our Lord and King.
To all of us, joy and peace, He brought.
To the angels declaring His birth as they sing.
He shows us a better way, if we follow what He taught.

Christmas

Devotions for Day 1

"All things are possible to him who believes."

Mark 9:23

When going through crisis and disasters in our lives or watching someone else going through trouble and hopelessness, we see some people turn to God and others turn away from God. We see this happening at Christmas, when stress can contribute to acts of hatred and unkindness. What has Jesus asked us to do to help these people? Jesus wants us to pray for them, invite them to church, and tell them the Christmas story about Jesus Christ. Do we take the time in our busy schedules to do this? We cannot through our own strength or reason cause faith in others or in ourselves. We can tell others about the gospel, and we can show them how to live a life dedicated to Jesus. At Christmas we can spread the good news if we seek out opportunities to plant the word through prayer, obedience, and trust in Jesus Christ, our Lord. Then others will indeed receive the hope they are looking for.

So how then is faith given to us? We are to give Christ the glory for our faith. Paul taught, "I planted, Apollos watered, but God gave the growth" (1 Corinthians 3:6). He also said, "So faith comes from what is heard, and what is heard comes by the preaching of Christ" (Romans 10:17). The Holy Spirit also does work to jumpstart faith within us. This Christmas let's pray for Jesus to bring our path to someone who does not yet know Him.

Prayer:

Lord, we ask the Holy Spirit to increase our faith. Let us seek out the fellowship of believers, especially so that we can be refreshed by each other and grow in our understanding of your word. Let us pray for others who are experiencing illness and hardship so that you can wrap them in your love, care, and guidance. Heal those that are in need, if that is your will. Amen.

Christmas

Devotions for Day 2

"Immediately the father of the child cried out and said, "I believe; help my unbelief!""

Mark 9:24

If I say, "I believe," I am filled with hope. Each Christmas we have opportunities to renew our faith as we celebrate Christmas. When we cannot accomplish something on our own, we need hope. To hope, we need faith, and faith is a gift we receive from God. In Mark, we read about a son, possessed with an evil spirit, who is brought to Jesus, as his disciples could not heal him. Jesus tells the father, "All things are possible to him who believes" (Mark 9:23).

These special evil spirits were part of Satan's plot to show that Jesus and His disciples did not have the power he possessed. But Jesus's mission was genuine, and the miracles were permitted by God during His ministry to show the extent of His power. Jesus's teachings show how important faith is for healing to occur in our lives. Satan was helpless against the power and name of Jesus.

In Numbers 21, we are told about a plague of poisonous snakes that occurred because of the people's disobedience and lack of faith. God instructed Moses to make a bronze snake and put it on a pole: "if a serpent bite any man, he would look at the bronze serpent and live" (v.9). Jesus makes a connection in John 3:14-15: "And as Moses lifted up the serpent in the wilderness, so must the Son of man be lifted up, that whoever believes in him may have eternal life." This year let's read these devotions and poems during advent and make a plan with each family member to honor Jesus in a special way.

Prayer:

Lord, we do believe. Help to make our belief stronger and help us to overcome unbelief in our life. Amen.

Christmas

Devotions for Day 3

"Make me to know thy ways, O Lord; teach me thy paths".

Psalms 25:4

"And without faith it is impossible to please him. For whoever would draw near to God must believe that he exists and that he rewards those who seek him."

Hebrews 11:6

When we come to celebrate the Christmas season, we find various colors used in the church vestments. These colors help us know what is being emphasized for that church season. The church vestment color for Advent is purple. Purple is symbolic of penance, royalty, and nobility. Hope and repentance are needed as we prepare for Christmas. The Christmas vestment color is white. White is symbolic of purity, glory, and truth; they describe Jesus. For Christians it means the restoration of innocence by salvation through faith in Jesus.

As the Lord teaches us His ways, we learn to live more effectively for Him, which leads to more peace and joy as we follow Him. Hebrews 11 discusses people known for their faith such as Moses, Abraham, Noah, Joseph, and the prophets. It is believed it was written seven to ten years before the destruction of Jerusalem in 70 A.D. by an unknown author. One of the heresies spread in several of the early churches was that the resurrection did not occur. Many were having their faith tested and growing in Christ as they responded to the upheaval in the church. Their religious practices were changing as sacrifices were no longer needed because Jesus, the ultimate sacrifice, had come. We cannot come to Christ without faith if we want Him to be our salvation, guide, and stay. This Christmas ask each family member if they would pick out a poem and draw a picture of their reflection of the poem they choose.

Prayer:

Lord, we ask you to be our guide, and stay. We are learning to bring everything to you in prayer. Thank you for the salvation you brought and faith given us by the Holy Spirit. Amen.

Christmas

Devotions for Day 4

"I can do all things in him who strengthens me."

Philippians 4:13

Paul witnesses to the Philippians by telling them he does all things through Christ and that Christ grants him renewed strength as he needs it for his missionary journeys and for spreading God's word of redemption. He had just received an unexpected offering from the Philippians. They were the only church offering to support him. They also sent Epaphroditus, who gave his personal services to Paul. Everywhere that Paul went, he was making converts for Jesus. He was stoned, but he sang in prison. He was beaten, but he rejoiced in his chains. He had learned that in whatever state he found himself, he should be contented and forbearing. And the Lord filled him with great energy to do his work.

Paul told the Philippians that they will share in the rewards of his work because of their contribution to him. This is also true of us today if we support the Lord's army of missionaries. Philippians 4:13 has a promise for us that all is possible through Jesus. Its promise helped me face many of life's uncertainties. We don't often think of the uncertainties that surrounded the birth of Jesus because the people involved in the Christmas story were indeed special . . . because of their faith. In Matthew 17:20, Jesus told the disciples they could not cure a child's illness because of their little faith. Do we also have too little faith to stand up for or do the will of God?

Prayer:

Help us to be grateful for the faith you have given us, dear Lord, and to be content in whatever place you have put us. Increase our faith as it is your will for our lives. Amen

Christmas

Devotions for Day 5

"But earnestly desire the higher gifts. And I will show you a still more excellent way."

1 Corinthians 12:31

We celebrate the birth of Jesus Christ, our Savior, each Christmas. If we slow our Christmas activities down, we may find time to realize how much God loves us. This love never fades. God sent Jesus to earth so that people would know God's true character through Him. When we ask forgiveness, we receive His mercy, and the split that occurred between God and man is healed. We become His children again. As 1 Corinthians 13:2 says, "If I have prophetic powers, and understand all mysteries and all knowledge; and if I have all faith, so as to remove mountains, but have not love, I am nothing."

We still worry and fret about how we will get into heaven with our deeds and how we can please Jesus. We need a time when we can become like little children singing that song "Jesus Loves Me." This is what Christmas is all about. He may not answer all our prayers the way we want them answered, but we know He loves us, having done marvelous things for us.

Christmas should be a time of greatest joy because our Savior has come and will work out salvation for us. He has indeed rescued us from Satan. Without love, none of the other gifts given by the Holy Spirit make any difference. This heavenly love is the most powerful force in the world. Love in action speaks louder than words.

Prayer:

Dear Father in heaven, keep us always in your care. Thank you for showing us a better way to live. Thank you for your love and for being in control of this world and of our lives. Let us use our energy in ways that please you each Christmas. Amen.

Christmas

Devotions for Day 6

"Neither death, nor life, nor angels, nor principalities, nor things present, nor things to come, nor powers, nor height, nor depth, nor anything else in all creation, will be able to separate us from the love of God in Christ Jesus our Lord."

Romans 8:38-39

Paul wrote this letter to give the Roman Christians a written explanation of the gospel. He taught we are to do everything we can to live as Jesus would have us live. He reassures "We know that in everything God works for good with those who love him, who are called according to his purpose" (Romans 8:28). Paul explains that the love of this baby Jesus is unyielding and strong. What a reason to celebrate joyfully each Christmas. He died forgiving us so that we might have eternal life in Him. This love is invincible and elevated above human love. If we belong to Christ, nothing can separate us from this sacred love.

If we look carefully, we can see that all nature is praising God. We find how wisely creation was prepared and how much God must have loved us. We see the following signs at Christmas. The Christmas tree's top branch points upward as if especially prepared for the star, which is usually placed there, leading to Jesus. It is as if God has arranged to make the time of His Son's birth extra beautiful for us. Nature is brought indoors. The Christmas lights, the Christmas trees, and the other decorations all take on a radiance that we long remember as we celebrate that Jesus Christ, light of the world, has come to earth for us. Our focus is on praising God for His gift and what the giving is all about.

Prayer:

Dear heavenly Father, help us teach our children about your invincible love for us. Each year, help us find ways to make that Christmas special and unique in service to you. Amen.

Spiritual Readings And Devotions

"The Christmas Card"

One hundred fifty years ago in England,
John Horsely created the first Christmas card;
Hand delivered it too, and it was so grand
Soon Christmas cards were in much demand.

Sending Christmas cards has become so prevalent.
What need for us does it fulfill?
Some ponder why family photos are sent,
Wishing everyone peace and good will.

Sending out Christmas cards can be stressing;
Is it worth the effort I ask?
What messages am I sending
To make it worth the task?

Christmas cards are searched for in the mall,
Looking for just the right one to be sent.
We find those that are simple and small
And those that are large and elegant.

Do I choose my Christmas message for what it does say?
Does it make the love brought to earth supreme?
And do I search my heart if in doubt and pray
To make Jesus the center of my Christmas theme?

Why is this task done year after year,
Sharing the past year's news in sequence?
It can be drudgery and dull for the writer to rehear,
And also can be quite an expense.

But I realized as I wait in anticipation,
My Christmas cards to receive once again,
How disappointed I am to find only a brief inscription,
Not a picture or their yearly events therein.

So the answer is not elementary.
Ways to communicate grow faster everyday.
As the growth of email and cell phones becomes ordinary,
Some are saying, what will happen to the Christmas card today?

But each Christmas card is an act of giving,
Of saying, "I sure miss you."
It is also the thought of caring
And making others feel less blue.

So the Christmas card connects me to those I care about,
Giving the message of God's love when I cannot find words to speak,
Sending the message, you are not forgotten, don't doubt,
Thanks for bringing God's love and peace to me, which is most unique.

A Christmas card can bring hope and support we do accord;
Prayer for guidance and safety for the terrorism our nation faces, not dread;
And connection to the family of believers receiving strength from the Lord,
Sharing the message of Jesus so that the Christmas news might spread.

The Christmas Card

Devotions for Day 1

"Oh send out thy light and thy truth; let them lead me."

Psalms 43:3

The sending of Christmas cards offers us the opportunity to send messages of hope and of the love of Jesus Christ, our Savior, to many different people: neighbors, business associates, relatives, and friends, just to name a few. Through a Christmas card, we can help plant a seed in the lives of those not committed to Christ, and these people can be found everywhere. I have found some of these people in church; they are there for reasons other than worshipping God. Through Christ, we can be sensitive to the needs of others and find those wanting, alone, and suffering. With the help of the Holy Spirit, we can find opportunities to share with them your love and God's truth.

Those who want to stop the gospel are using the legal system of our country to prohibit our religious freedoms. This last Christmas, businesses were told that they could not say "Merry Christmas"; instead, the greeting had to be more general, such as "Happy Holidays," or better yet, they were to say nothing at all. More and more, some Americans have attempted to remove any message that brings to mind, Jesus, our Lord, and Savior. As citizens of the United States, we need to be aware of what the Bible says in 2 Timothy 2:12: "if we endure, we shall also reign with him; if we deny him, he also will deny us."

Prayer:

Dear Lord, help us to be sensitive to the needs of others but to always put you first. Let us be receptive and grow in your understanding. We ask you to lead us. This we ask in your name. Amen.

The Christmas Card

Devotions for Day 2

[Paul] "went from place to place through the region of Galatia and Phrygia, strengthening all the disciples."

Acts 18:23

Paul knew from personal experience how important it was for early church leaders to witness to and support each other. Most of this work was done in Ephesus, which was the center of the Roman imperial highway. God especially blessed Paul's work in this area, and large numbers of people who had worshipped the goddess Diana became Christians. Many churches were established in an area of about a hundred miles around Ephesus. This became the center of the early Christian world.

By sending Christmas cards, we can spend time in fellowship with old friends and families who may be part of our support systems. Sometimes, this is the only time of the year that people communicate with each other and open their hearts and express their care and love for each other. When feeling frustrated and worried, communicating with other believers can restore hope. The events of Christmas, of which sending Christmas cards is only one, can serve to reconnect us to the family of believers, where we can receive strength from the Lord. The Lord "makes me lie down in green pastures. He leads me besides still waters; he restores my soul (Psalms 23:2-3).

Prayer:

Dear heavenly Father, strengthen us to do your will. You work in ways we cannot see; provide us with energy to do the tasks you have for us each new day. When one door closes, make a new way for us. Help us believe. In Jesus' name we pray. Amen.

The Christmas Card

Devotions for Day 3

"Nevertheless I tell you the truth: it is to your advantage that I go away, for if I do not go away, the Counselor will not come to you; but if I go, I will send him to you."

John 16:7

Jesus tells His disciples that He will send the Holy Spirit to them to comfort and guide them. God is working on our behalf long before we know there is a need. Christmas cards have provided me with the nourishment needed to strengthen my faith and to help make Jesus the center of my Christmas. I believe that words of encouragement and caring included in the cards were meant to be there for me. Although they were possibly unintentional on the sender's part, the words and messages included in the cards were so helpful that it was as if the sender knew what I was going through. I believe the Holy Spirit inspired them to comfort me. In Psalms 119:130, we read, "The unfolding of thy words gives light; it imparts understanding to the simple."

As we grow older, changes can make us blue, and this can happen more frequently at Christmas, when we miss those who are no longer with us. So we need these Christmas messages even more at this time. Because of the decreasing income many older people experience, it becoming harder to reach out with Christmas cards. However, it is comforting to know that Jesus never changes. The Holy Spirit is still with us. Have you saved Christmas messages or cards that were meaningful to you? Put them on the empty pages in this book!

Prayer:

Thank you, Lord, for all the ways you have strengthened us over the years. I pray that we will be able to continue to spread the Christmas story and its messages. Thank you for an opportunity to make this book into a delightful memento which will be precious, inspiring, and lift up the spirits of our family and friends for years to come. Amen.

The Christmas Card

Devotions for Day 4

[Haggai] "spoke to the people with the Lord's message, "I am with you, says the Lord.""

Haggai 1:13

During this period, many Jews had been released by King Cyrus. They returned to Jerusalem and started to rebuild the temple, but their enemies stopped them. In the following years, many things went wrong. Haggai prophesied what God wanted the people to do, and finally the new king allowed for the rebuilding of the temple. However, this story leaves us pondering God's meaning of the word *temple*.

Jesus taught that all believers made up God's temple or God's church. My body is God's temple, and so is yours. Wherever the good news is taught, the Holy Spirit works in the heart of each person. God is building His church where the gospel is preached. There people may hear about forgiveness and be brought to faith through grace. Christmas card messages may assist in strengthening the church. Our emphasis for the Christmas season can make a big difference for each of us during the year. However, one day of attending church out of 365 days will not prevent the perverted use of the holiday season. Paul says, "For we are God's fellow workers; you're God's field, God's building" (1 Corinthians 3:9).

Prayer:

Let us seek your will, Lord. Let our Christmas practices be such that we find life for you to be full and satisfying. Guard our hearts and hearths; let them be yours. Amen.

The Christmas Card

Devotions for Day 5

"I thank my God in all my remembrances of you . . . thankful for the partnership in the gospel from the first day until now."

Philippians 1:3,5

This greeting was sent to the church of Philippi, which had been established about ten years earlier in northern Greece. Epaphroditus brought an offering from them while Paul was in a Roman jail. Paul found himself in a position where his words were seeds to plant the gospel in Nero's court. There, he was already making converts. Luke 8:11 tells us "The seed is the word of God."

Paul planted the seed taught by Jesus, who promised forgiveness of sins and never to cancel or forget His promise. The Bible says, "For I the Lord do not change" (Malachi. 3:6). Jesus blotted out all sins, and He remembers them no more. Do we celebrate Christmas in a way that shows we plant and water seeds for Jesus? Do our messages sent to others strengthen them? Do we bring hope, joy, and love to other Christians and to nonbelievers? The church of Philippi gave financial support in their partnership with Paul, but we can serve in many ways, as the Holy Spirit works to give us knowledge, keep us humble, and make us open minded. If we find we hate the Christmas season because of over stimulating activities and exchanging gifts that do not warm the heart, we need to make changes accordingly.

Prayer:

We ask for your blessing as we work to strengthen each other and spread your word. Let us serve you with our talents, which the Holy Spirit has granted us. Amen.

The Christmas Card

Devotions for Day 6

"The fear of man lays a snare, but he who trusts in the Lord is safe".

Proverbs 29:25

"For we walk by faith, not by sight."

2 Corinthians 5:7

Fear is ever present. It paralyzes, makes one feel alone and abandoned, and causes anxieties over tomorrow. But if we have faith, we know that God is the keeper of life and empowers one to believe. Ephesians 2:8 states "For by grace you have been saved through faith; and this is not your own doing, it is the gift of God." Acts of terrorism occur frequently in today's world, and it is important to strengthen each other. Messages about the love and peace of this season may help us become stronger in our witnessing and support of others.

The early church did not celebrate Christmas, as the celebration of one's birthday was a pagan practice. The birthday of Jesus is first mentioned about 200 A.D. The first mention of Christmas being celebrated on December 25th was in 336 A.D. Some churches and countries still celebrate a different date from December 25. The above facts about Christmas are reported in The World Book Encyclopedia (1979, Vol. 3).

John Horsley made the first known Christmas card in 1843 according to The World Book Encyclopedia (1979, Vol. 3). To make Christmas more meaningful, the message on the card is important. Does it portray God's love to humankind with timely messages to strengthen the recipient? Designing your own card at Christmas can be very inspiring. Isaiah 41:10 says "fear not, . . . I will strengthen you, I will help you, I will uphold you with my victorious right hand."

Prayer:

Dear Lord, help us spread the love and cheer that is part of your gift given to all. Thank you for the gift of your Son as my Savior, filling our Christmas with your joy. Amen.

Spiritual Readings And Devotions

"The Candlelight of Christmas"

A Son was born unto us sent from God above,
And so the Christmas story goes,
Everlasting Father, light of God's love,
Our Savior and guide for all our woes.

A babe was born unto us, named Jesus Christ.
He brought God's love to us by grace,
Showing us that God's love does persist,
Bringing light into darkness of each place.

This baby Son brought us God's love,
A love that is like the brilliance of the candlelight
Coming to us shining from above,
Gleaming its message so brightly in the night.

Candles are lit on Christmas Eve,
Portraying the light of His love forever.
This helps us remember what we believe.
From the light of His love do not us sever.

The light of one candle is so small
It barely reaches across the pew,
But as one lights more candles so tall,
A stronger light spreads; then all see Jesus in the stable too.

The light of God's love comes to me through His Son,
Where it daily is lighting my path.
As the next candle is lit, the spread of light flows on
Putting love in our lives, not wrath.

So through the birth of our Savior,
The light of His love comes to all every day.
All we have to do is accept it, evermore,
And I thank God for it as I pray.

The lighting of candles on Christmas night is such a beautiful sight
That out of the world's darkness that exists
Comes God's love, spreading further and brighter, in all its glorious light,
Brought freely to each by His newborn Son, who is Jesus Christ.

So the lighting of the candles
Has a special meaning to me,
And while sharing the music like those of Mohr, Watts, and Handel,
I light your candle and pass on the light of God's love to thee.

Written in remembrance of a Christmas Eve when children assembled a nativity scene, and during the lighting of the candles, the gradual brightening of the sanctuary allowed the congregation, at last, to see the baby Jesus became visible to all present. It put the focus of Christmas where it should be; on Jesus Christ, our Savior. So with the wise men, the shepherds, the angels, and Mary and Joseph, we were there celebrating His birth.

The Candlelight of Christmas

Devotions for Day 1

[Jesus] said, "I am the light of the world; he who follows me will not walk in darkness, but will have the light of life."

John 8:12

The Jews did not believe the message that Jesus had brought. Jesus told them that if they did not believe He had come as their Savior, they would die in their sins, in darkness. One of the worst things we can experience is to be separated from our Lord and Savior. Paul says, "the god of this world has blinded the minds of the unbelievers, to keep them from seeing the light of the gospel of the glory of Christ, who is the likeness of God" (2 Corinthians 4:4).

When attending a Christmas Eve candlelight service and observing the light spreading and getting stronger as the candles are lit, thoughts of His love for us come to mind. As one grows in Christ, there is no question that He is indeed the word and the light of our world. He is the light we want to follow so we can walk in His forgiveness, righteousness, and joy. Light stands for truth, righteousness, joy, and purity. I also think it stands for the immense love that God has shown us. Jesus brought this love to earth, and because of Him we have forgiveness, purpose here on earth, and a guiding light leading us to heaven. Take concerns about a more meaningful Christmas to Jesus, and you may be surprised at the ideas that come up.

Prayer:

Thank you Lord, that when we fall you are there to lift us up, forgive us, strengthen our faith, love us, and help us on our way through this life. Guide us through the dark times and let us find ways to show others your love, which reaches heights and depths that we cannot fathom. Amen.

The Candlelight of Christmas

Devotions for Day 2

"You are the light of the world. A city set on a hill cannot be hid. Nor do men light a lamp and put it under a bushel, but on a stand, and it gives light to all in the house."

Matthew 5:14-15

We are celebrating the birth of Jesus Christ, who came to this earth, sent by God our heavenly Father. He is a light to us that cannot be hidden; He is like a city built on a hill that is visible for many miles. *Light* is defined in the New Lexicon Webster's Dictionary (1989), as a source of illumination, the power to explain things, and brightness; as a verb it means to show the way. Without light we could not see; there would soon be no food to eat, no air to breathe without plants, and no heat or energy. This world God created would not be the same without light, and it would not it be the same without Jesus Christ, our Savior. So we can quickly get the picture of how vastly important and significant Jesus Christ should be to each of us. Jesus brings love, peace, and joy into our lives, not wrath. He has bought me by grace with His resurrection and forgiveness of sin, and by faith He has restored me to life as one of His children.

His light is given to guide me, to love me, to mentor me, and to advise me. Psalms 43:3 says, "Oh send out thy light and thy truth; let them lead me, let them bring me to thy holy hill and to thy dwelling!"

Prayer:

We thank you, Lord, for coming as the light in our lives to show us a better way to live. Thank you for your love and for bringing us your precious gifts and for the opportunities to celebrate Christmas in unique ways you have shown each of us to make Jesus the center of our celebration. Amen.

The Candlelight of Christmas

Devotions for Day 3

"For mine eyes have seen thy salvation which thou hast prepared in the presence of all peoples, a light for revelation to the Gentiles, and for glory to thy people Israel."

Luke 2:30-32

There are many Christmas celebrations that talk about the purpose of the birth of Jesus Christ. This church season is called Advent and includes the four Sundays before Christmas. Advent comes from *"adventus," a Latin word* meaning *"a coming,"* and the emphasis is on hope. During these four Sundays, we are reminded of the coming of Jesus Christ; each week an Advent candle is lit until all four candles are burning.

One of the most beautiful ceremonies of Christmas is the candlelight service of Christmas Eve. In John 8:12, Jesus says, "I am light of the world." As such, Jesus can be viewed as our guide, mentor, or advisor. The light of God's love comes to us all from our guide, Jesus Christ. He is always there to light our path. All we have to do is seek Him. The light of His love and His word comes to us every day. In Psalms 119:105, we read, "Thy word is a lamp to my feet and a light to my path."

Prayer:

The gates for witnessing for Jesus are still open. Help us, dear Lord, search for ways that we can help with this harvest through spreading of your word and sharing of the magnificent and overwhelming hope and love you have given and keep on giving. Use us as shakers of our nation to spread your word, if that is your will. Amen.

The Candlelight at Christmas

Devotions for Day 4

"For once you were darkness, but now you are light in the Lord; walk as children of light (for the fruit of light is found in all that is good and right and true), and try to learn what is pleasing to the Lord".

Ephesians 5:8-10

Candlelight services for Christmas Eve are an awesome experience. As each candle is lit, messages of hope or peace can be conveyed, and the illumination in the church sanctuary becomes stronger and brighter until one can see the nativity scene.

According to Isaiah 60:1 Jesus is portrayed as light: "Arise, shine; for your light has come, and the glory of the Lord has risen upon you." From out of the darkness, Jesus, the baby, becomes visible to the congregation. Jesus is the light, and as He appears to us, we glorify, honor, and come to worship Him along with the shepherds, angels, and wise men.

This tiny baby, in all His glorious light, brings God's love to us. As we light our candles, we pass on the light of God's love to each other. However, there are those attending the service who are stressed over life's events, those who are apathetic, those who are hard hearted, and those who have their own personal agendas. By attending the service, we expose ourselves to opportunities to build deeper relationships with Jesus. In 1 John 1:7, John states, "but if we walk in the light, as he is the light, we have fellowship with one another, and the blood of Jesus his Son cleanses us from all sin."

Prayer:

As we come to church to give honor to Jesus's birth help us remember that God wants to know that we are thankful, and love Him. Even though there may be much corruption in the church we ask that this will not darken our spirits. Help us overcome and cleanse our hearts. Amen.

The Candlelight at Christmas

Devotions for Day 5

"The light has come into the world, and men loved darkness rather than light, because their deeds were evil . . . . But he who does what is true comes to the light."

John 3:19, 21

On January 6, the early church celebrated the festival of Epiphany. It started with honoring of Jesus' birth. The World Book Encyclopedia (1979, Vol. 6) tells us that after 300 A.D. the church changed the focus of this celebration to the coming of the wise men to see the baby, Jesus, who was the great light. This celebration commemorated the beginning of the spread of the gospel to the Gentiles, who were considered by the Jews to be the godless, the heathen, those who walked in darkness, and were separated from God.

In the days when Jesus lived, many people loved darkness rather than light because of evil deeds. This has not changed. Jesus said, "For everyone who does evil hates the light, and does not come to the light, lest his deeds should be exposed" (John 3:20). The Pharisees disliked Jesus so much that they were continually trying to trap Him into saying things that they could use against Him to kill Him. But Jesus, who was the great light, "gives us the victory through our Lord Jesus Christ" (1 Corinthians 15:57). Our gift is the forgiveness of sins He won over sin, death, and the power of the devil. We are granted this gift, freely given by grace through faith in Jesus.

Prayer:

Lord, we thank you for coming to earth so we do not need to be separated from the guiding light and love of Jesus Christ. Help us seek ways to spread your gospel to those who are living in darkness, not just at Christmas, but during the entire year. Amen.

The Candlelight of Christmas

Devotions for Day 6

"The Lord is my light and my salvation, whom shall I fear?"

Psalms 27:1

The psalmist, David, praises the Lord, who gives him light and strength. David grew up as a shepherd, tending his father's flocks near Bethlehem. It is speculated that the shepherds who came to honor the baby Jesus at his birth were from the same area. David was honored for his bravery, but after becoming king of Israel he fell into sin, as his character had become weakened by idleness. People were trying to kill him, and he lived like an outlaw on the run and in hiding. However, he loved God and repented.

There are many things to fear in this world: illnesses, wicked people, enemies, the darkness of night, death, not having enough money or food, and natural and man caused disasters, to name just a few. But God provides a place for us and out of the darkness of this world comes God's love for you and me through the birth of Jesus. God continues to bring light into my life; He daily lights my path. He has already demonstrated His love for me, and has become my guide and protector. The Bible also states in Galatians 3:26-29 that we are brought unto Christ that we may be justified by faith and receive the salvation that is there for all of us, freely given. Let us pass on the Christmas story, as Jesus works in our hearts, to those who do not know Jesus but especially to our families and others that Jesus puts in our path this Christmas.

Prayer:

We ask, dear heavenly Father, strengthen us so we are obedient to your will. Sustain us, and let us show your love to others. Thank you for being my guide and my protector even when I do not deserve this. We ask that this book be used to your honor and glory. Amen.

Your Gift From Heaven

The Light of the World
Shepherding Us to A Better Way of Living
Visible at the Stable, but Always with Us
Possessing Omnipresence So We Cannot See Him
Showing Us a Way to Eternal Life

. . . . Give Love and Thanks for This Gift Throughout the Year.

Notes from readings/discussions

Notes from readings/discussions

Notes from readings/discussions

Notes from reading/discussions

Notes from reading/discussions